Beyond the Subject

SUNY series in Contemporary Italian Philosophy
———————
Silvia Benso and Brian Schroeder, editors

Beyond the Subject
Nietzsche, Heidegger, and Hermeneutics

Gianni Vattimo

Translated, edited, and with an introduction by
Peter Carravetta

Original Italian edition: *Al di là del soggetto: Nietzsche, Heidegger e l'ermeneutica* (Milan: Feltrinelli, 1981)

Published by State University of New York Press, Albany

© 2019 State University of New York

All rights reserved

No part of this book may be used or reproduced in any manner whatsoever without written permission. No part of this book may be stored in a retrieval system or transmitted in any form or by any means including electronic, electrostatic, magnetic tape, mechanical, photocopying, recording, or otherwise without the prior permission in writing of the publisher.

For information, contact State University of New York Press, Albany, NY
www.sunypress.edu

Library of Congress Cataloging-in-Publication Data

Names: Vattimo, Gianni, 1936– author.
Title: Beyond the subject : Nietzsche, Heidegger, and hermeneutics / Gianni
   Vattimo : translated, edited, and with an introduction by Peter Carravetta.
Other titles: Al di là del soggetto. English
Description: Albany : State University of New York, 2019. | Series: SUNY
   series in contemporary Italian philosophy | Includes bibliographical
   references and index.
Identifiers: LCCN 2018021845 | ISBN 9781438473819 (hardcover : alk. paper) |
   ISBN 9781438473826 (pbk. : alk. paper) | ISBN 9781438473833 (ebook)
Subjects: LCSH: Nietzsche, Friedrich Wilhelm, 1844–1900. | Heidegger, Martin,
   1889–1976.
Classification: LCC B3317 .V35913 2019 | DDC 193—dc23
LC record available at https://lccn.loc.gov/2018021845

10 9 8 7 6 5 4 3 2 1

Contents

Translator's Preface — vii

Translator's Introduction: The End(s) of Subjectivity and the Hermeneutic Task — ix
    Peter Carravetta

Author's Preface: The Bottle, the Net, the Revolution, and the Tasks of Philosophy: A Dialogue with *Lotta Continua* — xxix

Chapter 1   Nietzsche, Beyond the Subject — 1

Chapter 2   Towards an Ontology of Decline — 17

Chapter 3   Heidegger and Poetry as Decline of Language — 35

Chapter 4   Outcomes of Hermeneutics — 49

Appendix 1   The Crisis of Subjectivity from Nietzsche to Heidegger — 67

Appendix 2   Hermeneutics as *Koine* — 83

Notes — 93

References — 105

Index of Names — 111

Index of Terms — 115

Translator's Preface

The present translation of Gianni Vattimo's *Al di là del soggetto*—literally *Beyond the Subject*, originally published by Feltrinelli of Milan in their series "Opuscoli" in January 1981—was conducted on the basis of the first edition of the reissue of the book in the series "Idee," in April 1984. The first draft of the translation was ready by the mid-1990s and was supposed to be published by Humanities Press in a series directed at the time by Hugh Silverman. It had been read by fellow philosophers Ron Scapp and Edith Wyschogrod. Unfortunately several factors contributed to its delay and when that venue proved to be impractical, the translation ended in the proverbial drawer. I am grateful to Silvia Benso and Brian Schroeder for accepting it to publish in the SUNY Press series Contemporary Italian Philosophy. *Al di là del soggetto* (*Beyond the Subject*) is a major contribution to studies of Nietzsche and Heidegger, and is a pivotal text in the development of the thought of Gianni Vattimo.

In preparing this version, I went over the earlier rendition and profited greatly by a close reading done by Silvia Benso, who insisted I stay close to the original where I had often preferred legibility or idiomaticity. Vattimo makes extensive use of German words when they refer specifically to Nietzsche and Heidegger's works, and I have retained those. On the technical front, I originally had distinguished between rendering *essere* with Being and *essere* (of humans, or of *enti*, entities) with being, whereas now the community no longer capitalizes Heidegger's key notion. Nevertheless, Vattimo distinguishes between *Dasein* and *esserci*, the Italian equivalent. When he uses *Dasein* it is usually with Heidegger's technical vocabulary in mind, and it is left in the German. When he uses *esserci* he clearly is not referring to Heidegger exclusively, but to the notion in a more general sense, or his own sense, and so I have often rendered it with the old-fashioned and literal expression "being-there." Italian words or expressions that are key points in Vattimo's interpretation, or have a broad semantic envelope and could have been rendered in a number of ways, are often added in square brackets, insofar as some readers may want to interpret them differently than the way I did. All italics are in the original, except of course in my own Introduction. I have also rendered *uomo*, literally "man," with "human being/s." For Vattimo's references to Nietzsche's texts in the Colli-Montinari critical edition and translation into Italian, I tried where possible to find corresponding English or German versions.

With the series editors, and with Vattimo's consent, we decided to include two papers not contained in the original *Al di là del soggetto*, mostly owing to the fact that they expand upon the same themes addressed throughout the book. The first, here as Appendix I, "Crisis of Subjectivity from Nietzsche to Heidegger," appeared in the premier issue of the journal *DIFFERENTIA review of Italian thought*, which I launched in 1986 (5–21). The second, here as Appendix II, "Hermeneutics as Koine," appeared in the journal *Theory, Culture & Society* (London: 1988, vol. 5, nos. 2–3, 399–408).

I would like to thank my assistant Soren Whited for his scrupulous reading and questioning of the many solutions I had adopted. A word of thanks also goes to Andrew Kenyon of SUNY Press and Jack Donner and Jenn Bennett-Genthner for the final copyediting and inevitable but crucial corrections and suggestions to improve the final product. But all translations are my own ultimately, and I take responsibility for any deviation or idiosyncrasy the reader may encounter.

Publication of this volume was made possible in part thanks to the support of the Alfonse M. D'Amato Chair in Italian and Italian American Studies at Stony Brook University.

Translator's Introduction

The End(s) of Subjectivity and the Hermeneutic Task

Peter Carravetta

Limine

Man is a mode of being which accomodates that Dimension . . .—always open, never finally delimited, yet constantly traversed—which extends from a part of himself not reflected in a *cogito*, to the act of thought by which he apprehends that part; and which, in the inverse direction, extends from that pure apprehension to the empirical clutter, the chaotic accumulation of contents, . . . the whole silent horizon of what is posited in the sandy stretches of non-thought.

—Michel Foucault, *The Order of Things: An Archaeology of the Human Sciences*

My hypothesis: The subject as multiplicity.

—Friedrich Nietzsche, *The Will to Power*

The question of the subject—its nature, origin, sense, possibilities—has been at the core of a great deal of critical reflection for the greater part of the past century, across a variety of disciplines, and snaking through different traditions and cultures. In literature as in politics, in the visual arts as in the various branches of philosophy, the late modern period of Western society has been witness to profound, problematic, uncanny crises in addressing the constitution, meaning, and manifestations of human subjectivity.[1] The subject has been the great thorn on the side of idealists and materialists, utopists and cynics, atheists and skeptics. Modernity, in brief, has suffered hermeneutic contortions every time it turned its spectacles toward this key notion, or very essence, variously articulated in distinct historical contexts, beginning with the Cartesian *cogito*, then framed as the transcendental self, subsequently as the (ever suspicious) unconscious *ego*, reaching the structuralist autonomous subject, finally as the ancient *figura* of the *theōrós*, witness and participant to virtual theorizing. It becomes patent how the fate of the subject will readily influence the destiny of interpretation.

Gianni Vattimo's work intersects and contributes to the rethinking of the subject at a point when the very possibility of the/a subject has already entered a near terminal phase, that is, when from various accounts and on the basis of utterly unprecedented political and scientific-technological developments—the post-World War II period basically—it appeared that what is at stake is not so much the unity, legitimation, idealization, and foundation of the subject—which had occupied thinkers from the Renaissance through the nineteenth century and created strong and unshakeable paradigms for thinking tout court—but, rather, how to deal with its manifest fragmentation, with its many delegitimizing embodiments, and with partial, incomplete or experimental versions. Moreover, the killing or overcoming or deconstruction of the notion of subject (and with it subjectivity) had been cogently explored in the influential works of Nietzsche and Heidegger.

In recent Western cultural history, the question of the status of the subject engaged in an oblique and insidious manner a host of other areas of inquiry and social issues. But, as we shall see in the following pages, we must be careful not to confuse the sense of Vattimo's aim, (and claim), reflected in the title of the volume, *Beyond the Subject*. The phrase can be legitimately read to mean something like "going beyond the subject," as well as, in a conceptual expansion, "let's think Heidegger, Nietzsche, and hermeneutics in ways not bound by our present understanding of the notion of subjectivity." In other words, this collection pursues the problem of the framing of the question of the subject *after* the obvious destructuration, destruction, deconstruction carried out by the two German philosophers, and what consequences it has, or can have, on interpretation.

On another level, the essays look at the process of attaining something not exclusively linked to the modern notion of subjectivity, suggesting perhaps a fluid predisposition toward engaging other theories, engaging the others, society itself. For Vattimo, the constant linking with the pre-conditions and/or the enabling strategies of interpretation assures a special, very personal investigation, such that in the end (at least for the period covered by these essays, 1978–1988) we can sketch a different kind of subject, one which has accepted the inherent nihilism that silently gnawed at the core of the Western metaphysical notion of being, and has also accepted the fundamental epistemological shift toward the endless reproduction and repetition of the technological worldview.[2]

This reconfigured subject is willy-nilly played out in a center-less, infinite network of possibilities and situations, and is found to be, in deep and enigmatic ways, driven to live, understand, and act in certain specific, meaning laden, accountable ways.[3] As we shall see, Vattimo never discredits the possibility that some form of reason may yet have to exist and guide our actions. It may all depend upon an act of faith—a systematic, and willfully executed plan. In fact, the dreaded exposure to nihilism need not be negative, need not lead to preemptive cynicism, to philosophical relativism, to digitized powerlessness, or to absurd chaotic violent paranoia. Vattimo's nihilism as revealed through the dissolution and reconstitution of the subject, of the concrete possibilities of a variously defined subjectivity, points toward a radical rethinking of ethics, of communication/community, of being-with-others . . . with a necessary (though alternative, tendentially post-metaphysical) sense of value.[4]

To explore and explain this complex path, I will sketch four areas of reference against which Vattimo's essays can be read. Of course, the reader may also contextualize their own ideas in ways not mentioned here. But that is consistent with the notion, accepted by Vattimo himself, that every reading, every interpretation, is principally a distortion, a *Verwindung*.[5] This appropriation/distortion, however, need not be thought of in aggressive, violent terms, as some sort of *Ur* fracture in being. Nor above all, as being wrong in some epistemological sense. It can also, Vattimo will argue, lead toward an open-ended, nonantagonistic mode of thinking, disclose new tasks for criticism and interpretation in general (Vattimo 1978, 17 passim). Finally, it can allow us to interrogate the text within alternative and postmetaphysical parameters (Vattimo 1983).

The possibilities are there, tangible and suggestive. Taking from near the destination of Vattimo's itinerary:

> The question on the "sense" of being, then, can be answered only by following the transformation of "sense" into "direction": searching for the sense of being, being-there moves in a direction which first dispossesses it, then de-grounds it (*lo sfonda*), and finally makes it "spring" or "leap" into an abyss which is that of its constitutive mortality. (See ADS 116, my translation)

One of the consequences for hermeneutics is to accept referents that are not grounded, unmoored discoursivity, chance, and the enabling force of linguistic interaction. Echoing Heidegger, what counts in thinking/acting is the movement, the trajectory, and therefore, implicitly, the *topica* experienced/developed to arrive at this and only this specific conclusion/beginning. There is in the background a rhetorical pact, a will to communicate and a coinvolving, interpersonal consensus enacted any time we wish to explain something to someone, anyone.[6] It is the intention of this critic, then, and implicitly harking to the subtle belaborations surrounding phenomenological hermeneutics, to explore the changing status of subjectivity and interpretation of Vattimo's background, the question of the interdependence between poetry and philosophy, the cultural relevance of the Nietzsche-Heidegger hermeneutic context, and explore/compare with other articulations of the issues by fellow critics, from both sides of the Atlantic, mostly from around the same years when *Beyond the Subject* was published.[7] We will then look at the notion of weak thought, and conclude with a note on what followed the present book.

Beginnings

Several of the themes developed in *Beyond the Subject* grew out of formal studies carried out many years before, in the late 1950s and early1960s, which culminated with Vattimo's first book after his dissertation, namely *Essere, Storia, e Linguaggio in Heidegger* (Being, History and Language in Heidegger).[8] It was published in the series "Sguardi su la filosofia contemporanea" (Perspectives in Contemporary Philosophy), no. 50, in

1963 by the Italian publishing house Edizioni di Filosofia (Editions of Philosophy).

Edizioni di Filosofia is the official outlet of University of Turin's philosophy department which at the time was directed by Vattimo's mentor, Luigi Pareyson. This is not an unimportant fact since Pareyson was one of the leading philosophers engaged in renewing Italian philosophical culture in the wake of World War II.[9] The climate demanded a definitive critique and debunking of Crocean idealism and historicism, most assuredly of Gentilian actualism. From an historiographic point of view, the young Vattimo found himself in the midst of a paradigm shift in philosophy, perhaps we might add against several background paradigm shifts, such as were occurring in the economic, the political, and the urban social spheres.[10] Philosophy and critique faced a confrontation with existentialism,[11] Marxism,[12] and finally Anglo-American philosophical currents.[13] Pareyson's contributions to philosophy in the fifties involved a personal interpretation of existentialism,[14] a re-reading of German romantic idealism, and the transformation of Aesthetics into Hermeneutics.[15]

In *Essere, Storia, e Linguaggio in Heidegger*, Vattimo begins by assessing the fact that there had been in circulation, especially in the post-World War II period, a substantial number of studies on Heidegger[16] which pointed to the crucial, radical relevance his thinking bears on the very practice and discipline of philosophy. He begins, significantly, with the chapter "Who is Heidegger's Nietzsche?" After briefly summarizing the two paths opened to metaphysics in the work of Aristotle and Plato, Vattimo proceeds to convalidate Heidegger's notion, as expressed in his *Nietzsche*, that the history of Being is marked fundamentally by a scission in which Being is progressively forgotten while beings (entities, beings as entities) assumed growing importance, authority, and (self)legitimacy as we move closer to the twentieth century. In this context, Vattimo agrees with Heidegger's reading of Nietzsche as the last great metaphysician who has dared to question the validity of truth as certainty, as well as the theologocentric, mythologized foundations of Being itself. This would make Nietzsche both, the last thinker in a tradition that begins with Plato, as well as the first thinker of a new or postmetaphysical epoch:

> In a loosely adopted Heideggerian framework, we can say that the substance of modern metaphysics as manifested in Nietzsche corresponds to the loss of foundation, the grounding

> being situated in the groundlessness itself, and which expresses itself in the will to will. With Nietzsche, with the disappearance of the distinction between essence and existence, there disappears also the last memory of the ontological difference which, although in the forgetting of Being, it nevertheless managed to make metaphysics possible. After him, in the history of being, metaphysics is no longer possible.[17] (Vattimo 1963, 23)

This requires taking a closer look at what happens after Nietzsche, while clearing the ground of the threat of historicism.[18] In subsequent chapters, Vattimo assesses Heidegger's contribution to the rethinking and recasting of the problem, delving in particular on the topics of temporality, being-towards-death, authenticity and the cruciality of decision, the then key issue of anxiety, the sense of nothingness, and finally the complex constitution of the event of Being, the *Da-sein* (Vattimo 1963, 75–84). It is symptomatic that Vattimo chose the *Nietzsche* volumes as a sort of turning point in Heidegger's path to thinking, but unlike many a critic and follower of Heidegger who believe in a major *Kehre*, a radical swerve that begins with the Kant volume, Vattimo consistently rethinks and relinks the thematic posture of the early Heidegger with the late one, understanding his path as a tortuous but ultimately coherent dynamic whole.[19] Only from such a profound closeness to Heidegger can he develop or unravel further, and from whose thought he could, as he will, distance himself (for instance, with the weak thought thesis) without necessarily betraying the German philosopher's insights.[20]

The Ancient Diaphora

In this context, reflecting on Heidegger's 1936 essay on "The Origin of the Work of Art," Vattimo sets up the stage for future investigations into the ontology of art and its deep connection with the eventfulness of Being. Vattimo looks at poetry as the privileged occurrence of the disclosure of Being, and explores some of its consequences. Art reveals that Being has an inextricable historical component that effects a concretizing gesture or renders something as proof (for instance, as text, artifact, monument, tradition). At another level, art is a (re)presentation of the hiddenness and forgetting of Being, and locus of ontological difference. Finally, art expresses or reveals the originary saying, the founding word. Having assessed this, and by reading the dialectic of Earth and World in conjunction with the later conferences on "Hölderlin and the Essence of Poetry," Vattimo underscores the definitive abandonment, in Heidegger's very terminology, of the existential analytic of *Sein und Zeit*, in order to pursue the happening or givenness of Being as language, addressing a saying which is no longer a founding metaphysical gesture, the *Ursprung*, but rather a disclosing event, one world among many others, and an authentic historical expression of Being:

> In his long dialogue with poetry, which represents a great part of his speculative itinerary, Heidegger is led to perceive that such a disclosing force is rooted in the fact that poetry places things entirely in their authentic being, insofar as it allows them to dwell in the neighborhood of the *Geviert*. The opening force of poetry with respect to historical epochs is based on the fact that in poetry, understood always as the locus in which language manifests itself in the pure state, things are really what they are: their thingness does consist in being object of representations or the result of production, but in remaining within the aperture of Being allowing the *Geviert* to dwell in its vicinity. Poetry thus exhibits a cosmic trait, though not as an evocative property whereby whatever it speaks of it recalls the cosmos in its totality, but rather in the sense in which it constitutes a cosmos, wherein things are truly what they are and on this basis can disclose historical worlds. The cosmic dimension of poetry is reduced to its linguisticalness not because language is a sign of the world, but because it is only in language that the world worlds authentically and things are in their true being. (Vattimo 1963, 123)

This interpretation of the crucial role played by the coexistence, coincidence of the poetic and the philosophical, familiar to North American Heideggerians,[21] allowed Vattimo to explore the entire Modernist tradition of the work of art, and of the avant-gardes in particular, with results that will be useful to the historiography of aesthetics and poetics, art criticism. and even literary exegesis.

Though we cannot dwell here on his 1968 book, *Poesia e ontologia*,[22] some of its insights must be mentioned because they provide crucial theoretical support to the present collection, especially concerning the ontology of decline, and the formulation of "poetry as the setting of language." Above all, we should recall the confirmation, in this later book, of the groundlessness of Being and the open problem of representation that issues from this, a disclosure that will compel the philosopher to return again and again on how the manifestation of authentic being in history and society can be registered or accounted for. On the same path, Vattimo frames ontological poetics, or the hidden vocation of experimental art in the twentieth century, in an anti-metaphysical perspective, identifying a general epistemological rupture in aesthetic theory and consciousness. Finally, he retrieves a discursive aspect of art against structural immanence, exploring it in terms of an elemental or cosmological horizon,[23] in a way taking the prophetic impulse seriously enough to influence understanding, and interpretation in general, *beginning with* the oscillation between Earth and World, the collocation (*Erörterung*) of the *Seinfrage* (the question of being), and the cruciality of *Differenz*. This particular critical result will serve as the mainspring behind other writings by Vattimo which bring the very meaning and authenticity of hermeneutics in indissoluble bond with the linguistic and rhetorical aspect of the human dimension. The essay presented here as chapter three on poetry as the setting of language can be read profitably against other articles that map out the profound and complex relationship between poetry and philosophy, history and narration, the power of the image and the necessity to cast out for meaning through icons, *figuras*, allegories.

The Nietzsche-Heidegger Knot

It would take too long and it would be out of place to recount the entire history of Nietzsche and Heidegger's influence on twentieth-century thought. But a sampling of its representative moments may be kept in mind as we attempt to understand in what ways Vattimo's *Beyond the Subject* is a unique and potentially radical critique of the notions of subjectivity and interpretation at the end of the twentieth century. Let us then recall also that in the Italian cultural panorama we are witness to a rich exchange on the constitution of the subject in epistemological, historical and political terms.[24] Limiting ourselves to the Nietzsche–Heidegger community, among the leading interlocutors for Vattimo during the late 1960s and through the 1970s we recall, from the Nietzsche renaissance side, the work of scholars and thinkers like Giorgio Colli and Martino Montinari, Massimo Cacciari, Ferruccio Masini, Fulvio Semerari, Giorgio Penzo, Giangiorgio Pasqualotto, Emanuele Severino, and others. Retrospectively, one thing is clear: Nietzsche was being read primarily against two discursive formations: Marxism (Lukacs especially) and Idealism (the Crocean version in particular). As becomes especially cogent in the *Lotta Continua* interview that opens this collection, Vattimo was very much committed to reframing the question by bringing his studies on Heidegger to bear on the Marxist challenge. At the same time, however, he was effecting a reading of Nietzsche through Heidegger's reflection on language, being and art. The result was his preliminary *Ipotesi su Nietzsche* (A Reading of Nietzsche) (1967). Compelled and willing to respond to and account for the growing untenability of the Marxist conception of the subject—for its being socially predetermined, for its excessive scientific claims, for the grounding assumption or the dynamics of power and antagonism through which it was displayed—Vattimo elaborates a configuration straddling the Modern–Postmodern divide, a dynamic, unstable, but ultimately creative and fluid notion of subjectivity.

A few years later, in *Il soggetto e la maschera. Nietzsche e il problema della liberazione* (1974), Vattimo interprets Nietzsche as the thinker of the defining crisis in the parabola of metaphysical subjectivity which ushers a self-regenerating, Dyonisiac notion of humankind, one which envisions a Zarathustra somewhat more humble and down to earth, an individual capable above all of overcoming oneself. But this subject is not reconciled in any reassuring and all-encompassing unity, and cannot be made to conform to the laws of dialectics exclusively.

Moreover, the Nietzschean revelation concerning the superficiality of the Modern subject, and the complementary revaluation of the body, the senses, the positioning of the now partial and unmoored thinking being, permits Vattimo to engage the reality wherein these forces interact, and maintain the Heideggerian perspective on Being towards death. In fact, "the disempowered subject should now be capable of entertaining a less dramatic relation with its mortality" (Vattimo 1980, 10). In the background, the enabling or signifying link consists of difference-degrounding-mortality.[25] It is interesting to note, in this context, that the

"French Nietzsche,"[26] which represented a diverse but somehow interconnected cluster of critics and had a definite impact in the United States, did not have an equivalent or parallel influence in Italy,[27] although the French thinkers were usually quickly translated and discussed in various academic and public arenas all the time.[28]

On the other hand, the reader of Vattimo's seminal papers on subjectivity and hermeneutics must bear in mind also an even greater, deeper, more complex Heidegger Renaissance in Italy, beginning with Pietro Chiodi's translation of *Being and Time* in the mid-1950s, and the highly individualistic interpretations which his thought spawned.[29] Much like twenty years earlier when he was writing *Essere storia e linguaggio in Heidegger*, here again the mid-1970s through the early 1980s there were new players on the field, and there had been in circulation several in-depth studies on the question of the status, fate, role of philosophy in general and interpretation in particular. We can mention here that important works by Massimo Cacciari, Mario Perniola, Ruggero Ruggenini, Carlo Sini, Ciro Vitiello, Eugenio Mazzarella, Pier Aldo Rovatti. Vattimo will read Heidegger through Nietzsche (see Appendix I: "The Problem of Subjectivity. . . ."), and he moreover will effect a few corrections or, better, necessary distortions, and finally urbanize Heidegger through a Gadamerian prism. In Italy, moreover, owing to a predisposition of the literary community to read philosophy, Heidegger has been partly responsible for the freeing of philosophical writing toward a more critico-creative mode, as can be seen in the period writings by Giampiero Comolli, Franco Rella, Aldo Gargani, and Stefano Zecchi.[30]

In their different ways, though, the multifarious intersections of these critical schools confirm Vattimo's historiographic characterization of the late 1970s and 1980s as representative of a hermeneutic koine, an association of diversified critical discourses which had as their main concern the question of interpretation, edging out the near hegemony of structuralism in the sixties and Marxism in the 1950s (see Appendix II: "Hermeneutics as Koine").

Contemporaries

In English, the number of conference papers, books and articles dedicated to the troubling issue of a fragmented and groundless subject are now legion, both in continental philosophy and in the human and literary disciplines. To take a sampling from those closing decades of the twentieth century, let's refer to Cheryl Walker, whose aim, in "Persona Criticism and the Death of the Author" (Walker 1991, 109–21), is to locate a reconstituted subject, a multiple or consciously metamorphic subjectivity capable of displaying a sense of (one's) self, no longer convinced that all subjectivity is doomed to indecision and autonomous play of signifiers (as per the French school from Lévi-Strauss to Derrida to Foucault to Barthes). This postmodern subjectivity does believe that its constitution and agency are predetermined by iron rules of social and material exchange (the Marxist view). For Walker what is required is the adoption of a persona criticism, a hermeneutic that discloses otherness without obliterating deep personal psyche and complex historical circumstance, a way (I refrain from calling it method)[31] of connecting and relating the creation of meaning by means of masks, whether self-imposed or encountered: "A persona is a mask that may be related simultaneously to the biographical data available about the author and to other cultural and literary voices" (Walker 1991, 114). The unyielding necessity to not lose track of both, the world as predetermined somehow and the subject as forever alien, suggests a focus on "patterns of ideation, voice, and sensibility, linked together by a connection to the author. Yet persona criticism allows one to speak of authorship as multiple, involving culture, psyche, and intertextuality, as well as biographical data about the writer" (Walker 1991, 109). The implication here is that the death of the author, of the sovereign intentioned subject is perhaps overdramatized, and that the recovery of some sort of lost mediation is yet possible. Within the horizon of the most dialectically engaging culture criticism, persona criticism does not necessarily oblige us to analyze texts and subjects by means of a thick description of sorts, although that would certainly prove a fruitful path. Vattimo himself, in an article titled "Difference and Interference: On the Reduction of Hermeneutics to Anthropology" (1982) suggests this possibility, insofar as a post–Heideggerian understanding of anthropology can disclose serious contributions to a rehabilitated notion of subjectivity which ultimately rests with human beings, men and women.[32] Nonetheless, what I find intriguing in Walker's hermeneutic is the assumption, at both a theoretical and methodological level, of the notion of *persona* as a *mask*, a *figura* that encompasses both the interpreter and the text, or the Subject *with* the Object, that is primordially aware of its function as a fulcrum, or a catalyst, or even an escape valve, in brief as yet another prism to read previously unseen glyphs, hear hitherto unheard sounds:

> What makes the mask preferable to the author as focus of analysis is the fact that the mask is unlike a human being. It is limited, identifiable, constructed, and without intentions. Indeed, in my understanding, the persona is almost precisely opposite to the historical subject-author in that it functions like an outline, a potentiality, rather than a fullness which is always already depleted as it renders itself in discourse. One might even call the persona a *thin description*, in the sense that it acts simply as a structuring mechanism, a predisposition that takes on substance as it becomes embedded in particular contexts. Furthermore, the mask is not a limit on what the text can mean. It is simply a feature of the text like a node from which meaning can be seen to radiate in many directions. (Walker 1991, 114–15)

This is pertinent not only to Vattimo's later overtures toward the specific exigencies of literary interpretation, as we find for instance in his writings on the "mortal essence of literature" in the essay "Ermeneutica e secolarizzazione" (Hermeneutics and Secularization, 1986).[33] But is also in tune with some of the fundamental insights of Vattimo's foremost teacher, Luigi Pareyson, whose notion of the persona has unfortunately not found many followers in Italy. Persona criticism is intended to be devoid of facile parody or pseudo irony, and may well be adapted to Vattimo's later reformulation of the postmetaphysical critic as *Übermensch*, a person aware of wearing a mask while aware of seeing the world through *that* mask. And yet, precisely owing to this apparent limitation, a subject all the more authentic, humble, and socially contingent. Walker writes that the masked persona is "necessarily artificial and therefore unlike human subjectivity, which, with all its artificiality, also produces the genuine one as one of its descriptive binaries. Limited and identifiable, the persona inevitably represents history, for its mask is embedded in ritual and culture" (Walker 1991, 119).

In the same vein, Walker's abovementioned notion of "thin description" as "a structuring mechanism, a predisposition that takes on substance as it becomes embedded in particular contexts" is not dissimilar from with

G. B. Madison's approach in *The Hermeneutics of Postmodernity* (1990). In this important work, Madison, adapting Emile Benveniste (after or at any rate beyond the deconstructions of linguistics effected by Derrida and Barthes), reiterates that

> language does not make sense, is literally meaningless, apart from what phenomenologists call 'lived experience.' There is 'something more' than mere texts and language. (Madison 1990, 165)

This obtains because "while there would be no subject without language, and while there most assuredly is no subject before language, the subject which does exist thanks to language is not *merely* a linguistic fabrication," *pace* Derrida and the deconstructors (Madison 1991, 164). The essence of subjectivity, says Madison citing Kierkegaard, is "interestedness," a desire to know (one)self in some way or other. Perhaps another way of expressing this is by looking at the rhetorical field as the existential a priori to all communication and interpretation. This would include what the speaking subjects, or agents of linguistic production, say (or think they say) about themselves, their rationalization of the sense of the self.[34]

Consciousness, too, therefore, is necessary, as it is in fact the engine of howsoever defined (or undefined) a subject we have at hand. One of the outlooks of hermeneutics, if we follow Vattimo, is that the interpretive process must allow for consciousness to express itself, respond to it, take it seriously once again, in short must retrieve past discussions about the what and whereabouts of consciousness. For over twenty years, entirely given to re-readings of the Nietzsche–Heidegger–Gadamer trunk, Vattimo has systematically avoided, in his writings, the very use of a philosophical vocabulary that harks to transcendentalism or existential phenomenology.

And yet, almost immediately after Vattimo publishes the essays gathered here, in 1983 he releases his landmark essay "Dialectics, Difference, and Weak Thought," where a postmetaphysical approach to interpretation and action recognizes the cruciality, in the age of the decline of the modern subject, of both dialectics and difference.[35] In yet other essays, Vattimo evaluates the importance, for a contemporary hermeneutics, of the contributions of semiotics and microhistory, vindicating the contingent yet constitutive and value-affirming traces, monuments, everyday implements that go into the lifeworld of the (however defined) subject, the human agent. This too, can be seen as a rehabilitation and recontextualization of a subject that is central to the process of understanding even after the fall of stable systems or Canons.

Enfeebling the Subject, Empowering Language

Developed parallel to the studies on subjectivity, is the notion of *Verwindung*, which Vattimo interprets as twisting, distortion, a "making recourse to" which is inevitably an otherness that foils any attempt at reproduction of the same, and thus a saying not exactly alike what it refers to. What applies to the understanding of (and indeed the relationship we have with) tradition, namely, that in its being handed down it undergoes growth or sedimentation or rewriting and is never equal to itself (except, perhaps, to pellucid rationalists), applies as well when we interpret our interpersonal exchanges inasmuch as each utterance needs to be complemented, responded to. But in doing so we are partial to it, we extract what we want or need from it, as we are influenced by specific phenomena and peculiar manifestations of the speaker in question, that other who speaks to me or to whom I wish to say something:

> The dialectical heritage through which difference is declined (*verwindet sich*) into a weak thought is condensed in the notion of *Verwindung*, and with good reason, for *Verwindung*, as we know, is the term Heidegger adopts in place of *Überwindung*, the overcoming or sublimation proper to dialectics. *Verwindung* (declination/distortion) and recovery ([*rimettersi*] recovery from, entrust oneself to, start up in the sense of sending on) mark the attitude which characterize post-metaphysical thought in relation to the tradition handed down by metaphysics. (Vattimo and Rovatti 2012, 46; Vattimo and Rovatti 1983, 21)

Verwindung[36] in short is the less than perfect interpretation we actually ever do, rest and rely on: it cannot pretend to be strong and absolute and universal and/or the master paradigm of anything: interpretation is originarily bound to the language being spoken/written, and moreover bears always an elusive element to it. Reappropriation is not possible without liberating being from the idea of stable presence, of *ousia*. But now we must ask: what would be a possible consequence of a reappropriation that no longer deals with being as stability? The answer is the enfeeblement of (the notion of) being. In fact, Vattimo argues, the explicit occurrence of the temporal essence of being "(ephemerality, birth and death, faded transmission, antiquarian accumulation) has serious repercussion for the way we conceive of thinking and of the *Dasein* that is its subject." This is the seed for the thematization, during those same years, of the idea of weak thought. In his own words, two years later:[37]

> To summarize, then, how a weak ontology conceives of truth, we could begin by saying: first, the true is not the object of a *noetic* prehension of evidence but rather the result of a process of verification that produces such truth through certain procedures always already given time and again (the project of the world that constitutes us as *Dasein*). In other words, the true does not have a metaphysical or logical nature but a rhetorical one. Second, verification and hypothesis occur in a controlling horizon, in the openness that *On the Essence of Truth* speaks about as the space of freedom both of interpersonal relations and of the relations between cultures and generations. In this space no one ever starts from scratch but always from a faith, a belonging-to or a bond. The rhetorical (or should we say, hermeneutical) horizon of truth is constituted in this free but "impure" way, analogously to the common sense that Kant speaks about in the *Critique of Judgment*. Bonds, respect, and belonging-to are the substance of *pietas*. Along with the rhetoric-logic of "weak" truth, *pietas* also delineates the basis for a possible ethics, in which the supreme values—those which are good in themselves and not because they are means to an end—are symbolical formations, monuments, traces of the living (everything that gives itself to and stimulates interpretation); hence an ethics of "deeds" ["beni," also: of "goods"] rather than of "imperatives." Third, truth is the product of interpretation not because through its process one attains a direct grasp of truth (for example, where interpretation is taken as deciphering, unmasking, and so on), but because it is only in the process of interpretation, in the Aristotelian sense of *hermeneia*, expression, *formulation*, that

> truth is constituted. Fourth, in this rhetorical conception of
> truth being experiences the fullness of its decline (as Heidegger
> understands it when he says that the Western world is the
> land of the crepuscle of being), fully living its weakness. As in
> the Heideggerian hermeneutic ontology, being becomes only
> *Über-lieferung*, trans-mission, dissolving even into procedures,
> into "rhetoric." (Vattimo and Rovatti 2012, 50; Vattimo and
> Rovatti 1983, 25–26)

Weak thought is an ample and supple dimension for thinking, as it allows for the coexistence and dynamic complementarity of different traditions, and Aristoteleans, Kantians, Nietzscheans and Heideggerians can find a locus for interaction, can be experienced meaningfully within our contemporary endlessly moving frames.

Consequences

Vattimo's reconfiguration of subjectivity and the new tasks assigned to hermeneutics can be read in parallel with, and found to be uncannily related to, an entire sector of the critical/hermeneutical community of North America, one which includes the New Historicists, Rortian pragmatists and Reader Response criticism. It can also be read as an addition to the panoply of notions of subjectivity displayed in Cadava's French offerings, *Who Comes After the Subject?* spearheaded by the semi-deconstructionist rhetoric of Jean-Luc Nancy (Cadava, Connor, Nancy 1991). Or as worthy interlocutor to the nomad and the feminist proposals on the destiny of the subject by Rosi Braidotti. And insofar as the work that followed the present collection is concerned, with its emphasis more on action than interpretation, on the living as opposed to the (re)lived, Vattimo's philosophical heritage can dialogue with the likes of Etienne Balibar, Cornel West, and Michel De Certeau. The affirmation of the mediating, channeling, or catalyzing role of the interpreter compels reflection on the dyanmics, the dialectics even, certainly the rhetorical/persuasive basis of interpretive processes and inter/actions. According to Stanley Fish, the precondition of some intention or orientation is at the basis of group identities and reader preferences. The meaning of a sentence depends on its capacity to connect, on closing (however provisional) a circuit. The critic cannot escape the fact his/her subjectivity is situated in between the sphere of the private and unique and the realm of an externally constructed language of self-definitions and norms.[38] Vattimo also appears headed toward this concrete need to articulate, again, yet again, humbly but undeterred, contemporary *figuras* for this private/public co-relation.

We must think, search for, or at any rate recognize what is "basically inaccessible." To do so when the interpreter becomes fully aware of the irrecuperable self-assuredness of the positing mind, the thetic construct of the mirroring critic. We can understand the predicament if we situate Vattimo's thought against a profoundly disconcerting state of affairs. With the demise of the subject, interpretation too is awash in irrelevance. In the words of Giangiorno Pasqualotto, author of a major 1985 commentary on an Italian translation of *Thus Spoke Zarathustra*, after Nietzsche:

> the critical intellect is no longer seen as . . . subject, as *ego*, as "I think" or even as a *res cogitans* capable of reflecting on, distinguishing between and judging the rupture between "pleasure" and "displeasure," but rather is grasped as multi-versum, as plural and polivalent phenomenon, as complex and never schematized web of impulses and rationalities, certainties and passions, instincts and self-awareness. (Pasqualotto 1980, 155)

The task itself is elusive, unsteady, perhaps too wrapped up in rhetorical constructs, in ongoing theorizing. In this perspective, a weak subject is not only possible, but a useful guide to navigate our millennium.

From these premises, it should not surprise us to read, in Vattimo's *Beyond Interpretation* (1994), that interpretation should not shun reason and rational constructs just for their own sake, that indeed hermeneutics can get by very well by accepting a circumscribed, non-obtrusive, nonprecategorical use of logical and normative linguistic constructs. It is consistent with Vattimo's other writings on the necessity, in the age of the forgetting of Being and of the compulsion to recall, to rememorate, celebrate, relate to, the residues and shadows of the great Western metaphysical tradition. Much like his contemporaries Derrida and Foucault, but in a very different language, Vattimo also accepts in the end the fact that we cannot escape our history and tradition, and that therefore what may have to change is not the premises for a Truth, but rather the articulations of an understanding, a tolerance, a willingness to risk the retelling of the tale all over again. And so why not employ some of the very tools or ruins or archives, ultimately, conventions, left around in the cultural (un)conscious? The Vattimo of the 1990s and of the beginning of the twentieth century is less interested in demonstrating how metaphysical reason(s) are irretrievably nihilistic and more prone to accepting some sort of median path, one in which action, intervention, and understanding of the relation self/others play a muted but perhaps still necessary role. So he feels compelled to save some of the categories inherited from High Modernism:

> hermeneutics must . . . develop . . . its own specific notion of rationality which, without falling back on the foundational procedures of the metaphysical tradition, would not cancel entirely the specific characters of philosophical discourse as distinct, for instance, from poetry and literature. (Vattimo 1994, 122)

The task of hermeneutics in Vattimo has shifted away from the earlier theories, based on the emulation of the work of art, from the thinking that might issue from an ecstatic, transforming experience, and is seen now staking new ground. It starts out by positing, as least common denominator, the exigency of a formal, socially accredited, metalanguage, or register, or style. A reasonable approach:

> hermeneutics can claim theoretical validity only to the degree in which the interpretive reconstruction of history is a rational activity—in which, in other words, one can argue, and not solely intuit, *fuhlen, Einfuhlen*, etc. (ibid., 133)

Consider now that the Vattimo who in the present book is theorizing the decline of Being, the necessity to "go-through" the master codes of modern thought, and take the risk of "overcoming oneself," is also preparing the terrain for a revaluation of the rhetorical grounding of hermeneutics, and subsequently of an ethic which goes "beyond interpretation." This is problematic, and may be a harbinger of his later swerve toward a reinterpretation of the Christian tradition, which deserves a separate exegesis as the very language he employs changes. Hermeneutics is always "the response to a message, the interpretive articulation of one's own belonging to a tradition" (ibid., 134). From this derives the facticity, the eventfulness of interpretation, the interpretive gesture which sets a path, which follows a destiny.[39] Therefore, besides justifying the valorization of its constitutive, enabling rhetoricalness, it also makes greater concessions to an interpersonally grounded hermeneutic wherein a certain notion of a self-conscious speaking—to avoid employing the term subjectivity—to and for others is entertained as being not only unavoidable but actually requisite.

One may wonder at this juncture whether the Vattimo of the 1980s and early 1990s may not have been attempting to bring philosophy *tout court* to one of its original vocations, that of being a discourse on coexistence, on living with others, an inquiry into basic ethics. To the view of Politics (philosophically) grounded on an idea (or archetype) of Truth, Vattimo now substitutes a politics which begins in a degrounded concrete present, in–the–coming–into–being, what he calls, with a richly textured word, *actualitas*, the ontology of actuality:

> Understood as ontology of *actualitas*, philosophy can express itself as an interpretation of the times which sets in motion an awareness concerning the sense of existence at this particular point in society and history. [But] . . . philosophy is not the expression of an epoch, it is an interpretation which necessarily tends to be persuasive but which is aware of its intrinsic contingency, freedom, and risk. . . . (Vattimo 1997, 123–24)

One cannot but recall the same or similar key words of another political season, one which struggled for decades with its philosophical counterpart, existentialism. An on that frequency we can hear the fully self-historically conscious view on commitment. Yet, at the time of the Hermes-like Subject and the growing importance of the linguistic act in order to counter relate to the forces of technopolitics and digital capital, the interpreter must explore other realms, genres, write-out in whatever way the being-in-the-(sociopolitical) present. The consequence of hermeneutics, therefore, seems to be a necessity, and a desire, and a destiny to continue forever to figure things and beings out almost *sotto voce*, in the age of the perennial distortion.

Author's Preface

The Bottle, the Net, the Revolution, and the Tasks of Philosophy: A Dialogue with *Lotta Continua*

Lotta Continua: Wittgenstein wrote that the task of philosophy is "to show the fly the way out of the bottle." Norberto Bobbio, in his book, *The Problem of War and the Paths to Peace* (*Il problema della guerra e le vie della pace*), uses the image of a fish in a net rather than that of a fly. Do you think human beings are flies in a bottle or fish in a net?

Gianni Vattimo: I'm afraid the idea that philosophy has something to teach human beings, something decisive enough to change their condition, is still part of an ideology that conceives philosophy in terms of a hegemony, an nth transformation of the power of Plato's philosophers, bound among other things to the Platonic separation between a world of authentic being—the outside of the bottle—and a world of appearance, of disorder, of inauthenticity. I prefer the image of the net—not because I see human beings as fish, however, but rather as acrobats. The net gets turned into a trapeze, a rigging, an entanglement of ways to be wended. Existence consists perhaps precisely in this movement along the meshes of the net, which is understood as a reticule of connections. There is no liberation beyond appearances into a supposed domain of authentic being. On the contrary, there is freedom as mobility among

---

This interview has appeared in part in the political paper *Lotta Continua* (*Constant Struggle*) (Rome, Sept. 20, 1981). Originally translated by Thomas Harrison.

"appearances." As Nietzsche teaches, appearances no longer go by that name though, for now that "the real world has become a fable" there is no true being left to degrade them into lies and falsity. The reticule, that net in which our existence is caught and given to us, is the cluster of messages humanity transmits in language and in the various "symbolic forms." I think philosophy should teach us to move in the entanglement of these messages, such that we live each single message and each single experience in its indissoluble tie, even continuity, with all the others, for it is upon this that the meaning of experience depends.

L.C.: What meaning can individual life or the destiny of the single human being have, what could be the meaning and destiny of humankind, in an environment in which "the future is not guaranteed," where we are passengers on a ship and do not know what port we are headed for?

G.V.: I don't think philosophy should or even can teach us where we're headed. It can only teach us to live in the condition of someone not headed anywhere. It seems more and more that the main mystification of ideology is what one might call the "Platonic fallacy"—the attribution of an eternal and stable character to being. On the basis of this mystification, knowledge sets itself the task of individuating truth, of discovering a primary principle, or a certain and definite point of reference—nothing less, in fact, than that place toward which existence is headed and from which it receives its directives (even the practical ones). But the place toward which existence is headed is death. Is this a pessimistic, desperate, nihilistic philosophy? I don't think so. Heidegger speaks of death as a "shrine," as a deposit of treasures. It is not only the relish for the things of this world that is tied to their precariousness and provisionality, their growing and perishing; even the richness of human history, which transforms and enriches itself (with significances, with nuances) through the vicissitudes of the generations and the multiplicity of interpretations, closely depends upon dying. Death is the shrine where values are deposited—the life-experiences of past generations, the great and beautiful individuals of the past with whom we would like to be and speak, the people we have loved and who have disappeared. Inasmuch as it is a crystallization of speech acts and modes of experience, language itself is deposited in the shrine of death. Ultimately, that shrine is also the source of the few rules that can help us to move about our existence in a nonchaotic and disorganized way while knowing that we are not headed anywhere. Our new experiences have meaning only insofar as they carry on a dialogue with all that the shrine of death—history, tradition, language—has transmitted to us. If the Platonic fallacy is refuted as being ideological and dogmatic, this continuity with the history of humankind—which we carry with us in language as traces, logical structures, and a priori forms of experience—is the only possible source of criteria, rules, and rational (or better, reasonable) directives that we can have.

L.C.: Is it right to introduce a better order through force?

G.V.: If what I said before is valid, this problem loses its meaning. A better order introduced by force is still conceived too much according to a Platonic model of true-being which, in its transcendent validity, would be able to justify the sacrifice of life, solidarity, and friendship, things that in contrast would appear to be mere appearances, negative values, and obstacles. Respect for what lives and has lived is the only "better" we know of, and this precludes the use of force. So then—is there no historical projectuality? No commitment to change? I must admit that, given the horrors produced by the great revolutionary movements, by the armed or unarmed prophets, I feel more of a commitment toward the past, toward the traces and values left behind as crystallizations, works, but also ruins by individuals who have lived, than I do toward an image-project to be formed for the future. Said in this way, though, this position seems too extreme. Still, I don't think it is absurd to think that such an attitude, which addresses itself more to the past than to the future, is paradoxically the one most suited to the conditions of late-modern existence. In a city like New York, where perfectly efficient skyscrapers are torn down merely to make room for new, more profitable constructions, the idea of projectuality as the particular trait of a free human being ends up in a crisis. Accelerated renewal is more properly the work of automatisms of the system—what becomes truly human is the care for what has been, for the residues, for the traces of the lived.

Today the future—the existence of a process, the occurrence of novelty—is paradoxically guaranteed by automatisms in the system. What is in danger of disappearing is the past, the continuity of experience, the concatenation of significations. Maybe that is what we should feel more committed to. The late-modern world seems even here, as in other respects, to be realizing certain Hegelian or Marxist theses by modifying and perverting their sense. For example, revolution as renewal seems to be a fact today automatically given in the system, hence in a way, it happens necessarily. . . . But then the conditions of one's revolutionary engagement changes as well . . .

L.C.: Max Weber spoke of an "ethics of conviction" and an "ethics of responsibility." What is the relation between these two models of rationality? Are we to believe that there are two types of morality, one "absolute" and one "political"?

G.V.: To oppose radically an ethics of responsibility to an ethics of conviction—or an ethics that feels committed to absolute values at any cost—means to accept a Platonic dichotomy between a world of true being (or value) and a world of appearance and probability. The value of Weber's distinction lies in its having made evident that such a separation is, ultimately, impossible. We need neither fanatics of absolute duty nor relativistic, accommodating politicians (to simplify the argument a great deal). The division reveals a situation in which the separation between existence and values still thrives. But such a separation thrives only as an ideological mystification, it is not a fact. Indeed, our own epoch is beginning to experience a world where absolute values and choices reveal themselves to be mythic entities, where, on the other hand, with the increase in communication, there are no longer pockets of existence that are absolutely insignificant. It seems to me that our experience bears witness to "diffused significance," which is undoubtedly less intense than the Platonic ideal of value and absolute significance, but also less dramatic, more extensively human. The polemic by a great part of the cultural world against mass society, beginning with Adorno, is probably also a result of the survival of, broadly speaking, Platonic prejudices. One doesn't succeed in adapting to a less intense and more diffused experience of value and so one brands such an experience inauthenticity, kitsch, manipulated degradation. Of course, the need for an intense experience of values is also a real need and hence should be taken seriously; but what it means perhaps eludes me. However, I believe that, generally speaking, the way for our historical humanity of the late-modern world to live and exercise its own human dimension is by developing the positive potential of a "declining" experience of values, one that is more diffused and less intensive. To return, however, to responsibility and conviction, I think that such an opposition should be overcome by an ideal of responsible action that neither limits itself to matters of fact nor proceeds at any cost but defines *with conviction* its own stances in a social dialogue (hence alongside the real possibilities of the situation) and also in a dialogue with the past.

L.C.: Is democracy a method or a value? Is it a method but not merely a method, content but not merely content?

G.V.: It seems to me that all this amounts to saying that democracy—if by that we mean an organization of society founded upon dialogue, upon a continuity set up through a dialogue of interests, opinions, and different life-experiences—is not merely a method but a value, in fact, the only value we can adopt as our basis. There are no absolute values to be realized by means of the dialogue and hence through democracy, just as there is no definite place towards which we are headed. The meaning of existence is to be found only in the experience of retracing the net in which we are caught and given to ourselves ad infinitum. On the level of social life and the institutions that structure it, this retracing is what we call democracy.

L.C.: Can a revolutionary end justify any means?

G.V.: I must admit I am not very clear (any longer) about what revolution means. I would ask in turn: Is there a nonviolent idea of revolution? One, that is, which doesn't involve absolutizing a value or a perspective (a class interest rebaptized as "the general interest" of humankind, for instance) and imposing it by force even upon those who don't share it? Doesn't the Marxist theory of revolution, as the affirmation of a class interest which is no longer a particular class interest—since the proletariat all of a sudden becomes humankind, the *Gemeinwesen* (communities), the generic being of all individuals—involve precisely an ideological absolutization of the interests of the proletariat into the general interest of humankind? We could reinforce this hypothesis with the fact that the assumption by which the interests of the proletariat are the interests of humankind has always involved a repression and normalization of the actual proletariats' concrete interests, which in order to appear as the general interests of all humans must be subjected to a violent labor of homogenization and universalization.

Moreover, if the Marxian theory of revolution is understood (as it is certainly correct to do) as the description of a process that, given the laws of development of capitalism, etc., cannot *not* occur, then one should object that, by the fact that it is actually inevitable, revolutionary violence does not thereby become a value to be accepted. As such, the task of an ethics might be, on the contrary, precisely to try to limit the occurrence of violence in any way—thus transforming revolution into a process of social modification that does not involve, or reduces to a minimum, the use of force.

L.C.: But if that is so, what meaning does the word *revolution* have?

G.V.: I think that in our language, for the most part it works as a symbol, as a coded word, as merely an instrument of identification: the really revolutionary comrades, revolution versus reformation, etc. What if we did away with it? Like war, revolution may be a residue of barbaric times, which will never really be able to inaugurate the new history of emancipated human beings.

L.C.: Is there such a thing as a philosophy of terrorism?

G.V.: I'm afraid that terrorism is indeed the most coherent revolutionary perspective. You cannot really attack terrorism by saying that the violence it performs is not rooted enough in the masses and hence not truly revolutionary. One can too easily answer that if there really is to be a violent revolution then someone has to start it, precisely through exemplary and disruptive acts of violence. No, the truth of the matter is that once you accept the idea of revolution as violence, as the assumption of an absolute value to which life, whether your own or that of others, may be sacrificed, then you have no argument against terrorism—it is right if it succeeds and wrong if it fails. But this is a most cynical way of condemning terroristic violence. There is such a thing as a philosophy of terrorism, and it is one that takes to its extreme consequence the idea that human history has an absolute norm, a final value to realize. The individuals or classes who feel (on the basis of evidence that is ultimately intuitive) that they are the upholders of this value acquire the right to pronounce life or death on all others. I am aware of the fact that fortunately not all utopians and revolutionaries are persons of violence and terrorists. With a little exaggeration, however, I would say that this is purely an accident. A metaphysical, absolutist relation to values very logically involves the risk of justifying homicide (on this, one should read the beautiful book by Emmanuel Lévinas, *Totality and Infinity*). Besides, without even thinking of contemporary terrorism, the history of social and individual repression is basically a story of values to which one has repeatedly sacrificed life (as in wars, martyrs, pogroms) or other essential aspects of it: the impulses, the quest for happiness, sexuality, etc.

The attractiveness of the idea of revolution, of storming the winter palace, lies entirely in the hope that there can be a time of absolute relation to absolute value, a time of identification between event and significance, between existence and the ideal. There are some verses of Hölderlin that say, "Only at moments can man endure the divine fullness. The dream of them thereafter is life" (in stanza 7 of the elegy "*Brot und Wein*" [Bread and Wine]). Yet these moments have always already vanished. The claim of having a relation to values that is not governed by memory, nostalgia, or cult is a demonic claim, which brings as its mark and consequence precisely the justification of homicide.

L.C.: But then if truth is not an absolute value, not an ideal norm of a Platonic type, what is it?

G.V.: To begin with, there is no reason to refute the notion of truth as a statement that is confirmed and proven on the basis of specific criteria of verification, therefore imposing itself as the solution to a problem or as the correct answer to a question. Even Heidegger, when elaborating his doctrine of truth as primarily "unconcealment" and not "conformity" (of the proposition to the thing and at the same time to the syntactic rules of a specific language), did not intend to contradict this first and obvious concept of truth. It is just that, as anyone knows who has read Heidegger or keeps in mind the Marxian theory of ideology, a statement is always proven true or false according to rules that are not themselves objects of demonstration. Rather, they are given to us, just as ordinary language is given to us, on the sole basis of which we are able to construct all the regulative and formalized languages. Truth, in a less formal and more profound sense, is if you will, a matter played out on this level. This is what Heidegger had in mind when he spoke of unconcealment—statements verified according to preestablished rules are true, but truth is initially the establishment, the opening-up, the historical and destined (because not an object of manipulation, decision, etc.) giving of the criteria on the basis of which true statements are formed and verified.

We cannot have a scientific relation to this truth. We cannot prove it or show it to be false through experiments. In fact, philosophy has always defined its own mode of access to truth by using such terms as *reflexive* or *transcendental*, alluding more or less to the fact that in philosophical statements we acknowledge the existence of structures within which we always already operate, and which even condition our becoming aware of them.

The novelty of twentieth-century thought, and in particular of Heidegger, consists in the realization that these structures, which Kant held to be the same for reason in any time or place, are themselves historical-forwarding (*storico-destinali*) events. This is what I had in mind when speaking earlier about the fact that we are caught and "given to ourselves" in a net, the net of tradition, of all that is transmitted to us in language, all that conditions and makes possible each one of our experiences of the world. Philosophy, as a way of reflecting upon, of returning to, these transcendental conditions of experience—which are historically mutable, however, as are language and culture—is not a science. It does not prove statements, it does not solve problems so as to proceed cumulatively to the solution of other statements, it is more of an exercise in mortality and hence to some extent also an edifying or aesthetic discourse, insofar as it makes no conclusions but rather intensifies and enriches our experience of things, complicating it with growing and degrounding (*sfondanti*) references. Hence we cannot say that truth (in the originary, philosophical sense) is such and such a thing. We respond to the question instead with a lengthy discourse and understand truth as alluding to this complex situation, to our being thrown (as Heidegger says) into a horizon of comprehension of the world inscribed in our language and cultural tradition, without, for all that, being able to identify fixed structures given once and for all (as, basically, Chomsky would like).

L.C.: This notion of truth and the kind of weight you attribute to mortality seem closer to Heidegger than to Nietzsche. In your book on Nietzsche (*Il soggetto e la maschera* [*The Subject and its Mask*], Milan:

Bompiani, 1974), you spoke of the coincidence of event and significance, the dance, the laughter of Zarathustra, social life liberating itself for a "Dionysian" production of symbols . . .

G.V.: The book on Nietzsche was written in the wake of the year 1968; and while I still think that the sections on textual analysis, on the explication of key concepts of Nietzsche's philosophy are valid, I now realize that the book, especially in the final section, was too much under the sway of dialectics. The *overman* of Nietzsche—as I proposed to translate the word *Übermensch*—was characterized there as a type of Hegelian absolute spirit or "disalienated" Marxian human being. That is, he was defined in terms of self-conciliation, of self-reappropriation, and hence necessarily (though only implicitly) in terms of self-consciousness. Rereading Nietzsche and, if you will, also living through the experiences of the movement in these past few years, I now think that the definition of the Nietzschean overman and his ideal of freedom must be more strictly distinguished from any dialectical perspective, and seen as less purely reactive. I would like to say that the "overman" is "over-" even because such a person no longer needs to realize that ideal of absolute conciliation, which seems to be the only goal worth seeking for the individuals of the metaphysical tradition up to Hegel and Marx. The ideal of reappropriation is still too reactively tied to the state of expropriation into which the Platonic vision of values, the separation of the ideal and the real, etc., has thrust human beings in the West. One might reach such a conclusion, which makes for a more appropriate reading of Nietzsche, even by considering the conditions of human existence within the late-modern world: the ideal of the subject as a reconciled self-consciousness, as a reappropriated self, has, I believe, lost its meaning within such conditions. Theories of ideology and the developments of psychoanalysis have alerted us to the irremediable feature of mask that clings even to this ideal. Moreover, the concrete conditions of life have brought to light the possibility of existing without being subjects of this sort (without, for instance, wanting to be masters, whether of things or of ourselves, at any cost). Today the possibility exists for new ideals of humanity that are no longer tied to the metaphysical concept of the subject. On this count, Heidegger's polemic against humanism seems to link up with Nietzsche's teaching. He said, among other things, that it has now become possible for modern human beings to think of themselves not each as an immortal soul but as many mortal souls. This is, once again, what seems to me to be the meaning of our new, possible, superficial, non-Platonic, experience of values and meanings.

L.C.: In the perspective you are describing, what possibility is there for a new history in which events carry their significance within them, which is not marked by what Sartre in *The Critique of Dialectical Reason* called the relapse into "counter-finality"?

G.V.: For a long time, I thought that the Nietzschean overman was the liberated subject (liberated, ultimately, even from subjectivity), capable of living experiences as finally identical to their significance, for the very reason that the new freedom that was to be realized, even by a revolutionary transformation of society, would have excluded any lapse into counter-finality. However, this still presupposes, as in Sartre's case, the ideal of *dialectical conciliation* as the meaning of history. Said otherwise, there is an encompassing meaning of history, an ultimate meaning, and the problem is how the individual subjects, by freeing themselves from all (not only economical) forms of alienation, could possess this global meaning of history as they live it. Though transformed, it is still Lukács's ideal of class consciousness on the part of the proletariat: the proletariat seen as a revolutionary class and, generally, as the anticipation of free humanity; for, present to its consciousness (illuminated by the avant-gardes and the party) is the knowledge, neither mystified nor masked, of the real meaning of history, the true and not ideological knowledge. And thus Sartre writes that our goal lies in drawing the moment near when history will have only one meaning, which will tend to dissolve itself in concrete human beings who will make history collectively. I would stress the term *dissolution* in a direction that certainly pushes Sartre's original meaning. The meaning of history cannot be identified with the actions and intentions of the individuals who act in it without that very meaning undergoing a process of dissolution. The real exit from prehistory does not lie in appropriating a so-called "absolute," teleological meaning of history (as dialectical perspectives still have in mind) but rather in recognizing that history in a certain sense has no meaning, at least no such meaning. The meaning of history then becomes something that can be had by whoever makes it. . . . Thus, whether with regard to Sartre or to Nietzsche as I saw him in my 1974 book (*Il soggetto e la maschera*

[The subject and its mask]), I think the time has come to emphasize this dissolution or weakening of meaning. It is what I think should be called an "ontology of decline."

L.C.: What does that imply? A "decadent" perspective? And how does it tie in with the proposal to think difference (which you maintain in *The Adventures of Difference*, Milan: Garzanti, 1980) as opposed to dialectics?

G.V.: What I understand by "ontology of decline" has nothing to do with a pessimistic or decadent sensibility or with some "decline of the West" or any such thing. It is, if you will, a rigorously theoretical discourse that deals with the manner of the self-giving [*darsi*; also: coming forth] of being in our experience. It seems to me that the principal teaching of Heidegger, and to a certain extent also of Nietzsche (the idea of the eternal recurrence), is that being is not what endures, what—as Parmenides would have it—is and cannot not be, hence even less become. On the contrary, it is precisely what becomes, comes to life and dies, and for that very reason has a history, a permanence of its own in its concatenated multiplicity of meanings and interpretations, a multiplicity that forms the frames and possibilities of our experience of things. The ontology of decline alludes to, more than describes, a concept of being that is modelled not on the immobile objectivity of the objects of science (and, let us not forget, also of commodities, removed from the realm of use and frozen in pure exchange values), but rather on life, which is a game of interpretations, growth and mortality, and history (not to be confused with historicist dogmatisms). This concept of being as living-declining (i.e., mortal) is, furthermore, better suited to grasping the significance of experience in a world like ours which no longer offers—if ever it did—a contrast between appearance and being but only the play of appearances, entities that do not have any of the substantiality given them by traditional metaphysics.

Difference relates to all this because the thinking of difference consists in the recognition that one can never have full "prehension" of being but only a recollection (the word is Heidegger's), a trace, a memory. Being thus conceived liberates us, sets us free from the injunctions of evidence and values, from all the forms of fullness dreamed up by traditional metaphysics that have constantly masked and justified authoritarianisms of all kinds. While freeing us, being conceived in this way also suspends us. It puts us in a state of fluctuation [*oscillazione*] (again paraphrasing Heidegger) which also seems to be what Nietzsche describes with the idea of "free spirit." Dialectics, on the other hand, always thinks in reference to a possibly full, final, or totalizing presence of being (even if, as in Adorno's negative dialectics or Bloch's utopianism, it conceives of this fullness merely as a regulative ideal) and, as a consequence, runs the risk of not freeing us at all (the developments of actual socialism don't strike me as accidental with respect to this meaning of Marxian dialectics, even if they probably cannot be deduced exclusively and necessarily from it). The point is always to see whether we can live free from neurosis in a world where "God is dead," where it has become clear that there are no fixed, no guaranteed, no essential structures, but really only adjustments. Yet these adjustments are not without some sense of direction. The tradition, the message that speaks to us in human experience, as crystallized in language, in the various languages, hence also in the technologies we happen to be using, this tradition is constantly disclosing possibilities to choose from and criteria of rationality, or better, of reasonableness. The condition that delineates itself in this way is not a desperate one, if only we manage to face it with what Nietzsche calls a "good character," the capacity to put up with a fluctuating existence and mortality. This—rather than how to find the way out of the bottle—is what philosophy may be able to teach us.

1

Nietzsche, Beyond the Subject

Georges Bataille's essay "The 'Old Mole' and the Prefix *Sur* in the Words *Surhomme* [Superman] and Surrealism" contains some of the most illuminating (and historically influential) pages on Nietzsche.[1] Here Bataille turns his attention to the meaning of the prefix *über*, whose sense is crucial for understanding the concept of *Übermensch*, which is central for the later Nietzsche. On his part, Heidegger also, both in his seminars on Nietzsche and in his essay "Who is Nietzsche's Zarathustra?" contained in *Vorträge und Aufsätze* (1954), places at the heart of his reflection precisely the meaning of "overcoming" implied in the notion of *Übermensch*, according to him one of the five well known *Leitworte* of Nietzsche's thought. These are but two examples of the importance that the problem of the *Übermensch* has for both the proper reading of Nietzsche and the recognition of its vast theoretical implications. Even the question of Nietzsche's affinity with the ideologies of fascism and Nazism, which for years weighted on Nietzsche studies, is tightly linked with the sense we attribute to the notion of *Übermensch*, as both the preceding and the ensuing discussion is based precisely on the question of the prefix. The idea of a Nietzsche precursor of Nazism presupposes, in fact, that the superman (*superuomo*)—or, as I believe we should say, the overman (*oltreuomo*)—can be portrayed in relation to a pure and simple overturning of all *Humanität* ideals handed down to us by European humanism.

The problem, however, does not concern just or primarily Nietzsche's position in the humanistic tradition of Western thought. It concerns also and perhaps above all his relation to the philosophic dogmas of that nineteenth- and twentieth-century form of thought that has condensed in an exemplary way the values of the European humanist tradition, that is to say, Hegelian-Marxian dialectics. Under the form of the materialist conception of history, to this day dialectics avers to offer the only valid interpretation of the conditions of human existence in the world, indeed it claims to be perhaps the only still feasible philosophy of history (and as such it is still widely practiced in our culture). It is precisely against dialectics that we must measure Nietzsche's effort to diagnose the evils of modern culture while suggesting some remedies. The question of the meaning of the *über* becomes thus a crucial factor in the discussion of the relation between Nietzsche's thought and dialectical thought (which, for example, takes up much of Deleuze's work).[2] This factor in turn is decisive for anyone who looks to Nietzsche with theoretical expectations—that is to say, seeking answers still pregnant with a future.

In our efforts to figure out the sense of the *über* that defines the overman, and with it the sense of Nietzsche's rapport with the humanistic and metaphysical tradition of the West, we cannot but run into the problem of the subject. I think there is reason enough to state that the overman of which Nietzsche speaks beginning with *Thus Spoke Zarathustra* can be characterized as a "reconciled subject" (*soggetto conciliato*), a subject thought within the horizon of dialectics.

We can speak of a reconciled subject provided we conceive of it as the endpoint of a movement of *Aufhebung* (resolution), as an overcoming. But this concerns consciousness, as in Hegel's *Phenomenology of Spirit*, as well as institutions, as in the *Philosophy of Right* and, more broadly and radically, in Marx's idea of the revolutionary suppression of alienation. Now, in a certain sense, Nietzsche's *Übermensch* undoubtedly manifests traits that bring him close to a reconciled subject. When, in fact, Nietzsche links him to another locus of his doctrine, namely the eternal recurrence of the same, the *Übermensch* is distinguished from the human being of the preceding tradition, the *bisheriger Mensch* (previous man), insofar as he no longer lives the tension between existence and sense, being and having to be, fact and value. Rather, he realizes in each moment of his existence a perfect coincidence of the two terms. The meaning of this can best be grasped if we think of medieval theology and its thesis of the coincidence of essence and existence in God and in God alone, whereas in all finite creatures finiteness is expressed precisely in the never perfect unity of the two terms. Nietzsche's description, in aphorism 341 of *The Gay Science*, of the individual capable of wanting the eternal recurrence of the same—and therefore of an individual who can be considered as the model for the *Übermensch*—is that of a happy person, someone who may want the repetition of the present moment because in it such a person experiences happiness, the coincidence of the event with its sense.[3] Seen in the context of a broader and deeper analysis, the eternal recurrence cannot be coherently defined in Nietzsche's text other than as the condition of an existence no longer severed from sense (Deleuze 1985 [1962]). In existence thus understood, the structure of temporality is profoundly altered. For temporality has always been experienced by Western human beings as a movement toward transcendent values, goals, and objectives, which confer meaning to becoming only inasmuch as they withdraw from it. Yet this coincidence of sense and event, which following our hypothesis is what Nietzsche is thinking with his doctrine of the eternal recurrence, can it not be understood also as just another name for the self-transparency of spirit as Hegel theorized and imagined it realized in (his own) philosophy? Or even, as another name to indicate the unalienated subject, emancipated from the division of labor and the fetters of ideology, as was expected from the communist revolution—so suggestively described, in the tracks of Marx, by Ernst Bloch in his philosophy of hope?[4]

If such a coincidence were to obtain, we could legitimately think that the Nietzschean overman, and with him the proposal of the rebirth of a tragic, Dionysian culture, are still bound to the preceding tradition by means of a rapport of dialectical overcoming which is suppression, though also conservation and fulfilment. Now, the most reliable definition of Nietzsche's concept of the *Übermensch* remains the one that thinks of him as identity of event and sense. There are, however, also solid reasons to believe that this identity cannot justify the identification of Nietzsche's *Übermensch* with the "reconciled subject" of dialectical thought. Above all, the *Übermensch* cannot be understood as a reconciled subject because it cannot be thought as *subject*. The very notion of subject is in fact the constant target of Nietzsche's unmasking of the contents of metaphysics and Platonic-Christian morality. As he writes in *Beyond Good and Evil*, paragraph 34: "Is it not permitted to be a bit ironical about the subject no less than the predicate and object?" This is an irony that, in Nietzsche's development, surfaces most strongly in his mature writings, right about the time when he is outlining the doctrine of the overman. This irony is justified by the superficial, non-originary character of the subject. One cannot speak of certain "things in themselves," writes Nietzsche in some note for the *Wille zur Macht*, because no things are given without reference to some horizon of sense that makes their self-giving possible. If this is how matters stand, we must then say that things are the work of the subject that represents, wants, and experiences them. Yet the subject also is something that is similarly "produced" (*Geschaffenes*), a "thing" among things, "a simplification with which to designate the *power* which posits, invents, experiences, distinguishing it from all other single positing, inventing, even thinking. That is, the faculty characterized in its difference from any particular. Ultimately, doing (*fare*) understood from the point of view of all the doing which we might still expect."[5]

A power, however, he writes in another entry from the same period, "has not yet been able to come into being as such, what we get rather are its effects. But when these are marked as effects of a power they are as if translated into a completely different language."[6]

In these and similar texts, one can gauge Nietzsche's distance from any sort of empirical or transcendental idealism, as well as from any dialectical perspective. The power or force which we discover underneath the traditional notion of the subject is nothing comparable to the transcendental subject and its being distinct from the empirical subject, which makes it possible for dialectics—or for history itself—to exist as process of progressive identification of the two terms. For Nietzsche, the very term power is already a translation, or better: power is given only through its *Wirkungen*, which are ultimately translations. With respect to effects, the pointing to a power, a *Vermögen* which remains while distinguishing itself from all its changeable positions, is once again but an act of translation, a metaphor. Everything happens according to Nietzsche's example in a page from *Twilight of the Idols*. A distant cannon shot is heard while sleeping; in the dream, we link it to a story which *a posteriori* seems to be its cause and explanation.[7] Now, the will, consciousness, and the I as causes or subjects of what we happen to be doing or suffering, "are merely after-products, obtained after causality had, on the basis of will, been firmly established as a given fact, as *empiricism*" (*Twilight of the Idols*, par. 3). The subject is not a *primum* to which we can dialectically return, for it is itself a surface effect and, as the same paragraph states, has become "a fiction, a play on words." It could not be, or it did not have to be, considered as such (a fiction) for a long period in our history because at a certain point in this story "causality established itself as given." Much like the other great errors of metaphysics and morality, belief in the I also goes back, by means of the belief in causality, to the will to find someone responsible for the events. The structure of language and above all the grammar of subject and predicate, of subject and object, together with the notion of being that metaphysics has built on such a structure (with principles, causes, etc.), is entirely modeled on the neurotic need to attribute a responsibility to becoming (ibid., par. 8). But "meanwhile we have thought better. Today we do not believe a word of it" (ibid., par. 3). The "meanwhile" to which Nietzsche refers here stands for the entire arc of the history of thought in which the constitution and destitution of metaphysics is consumed: It is that history of the death of God which makes superfluous any ultimate explanation, principles, and even the responsible subject. Dominated by the category of *Grund* (foundation), the universe of metaphysics is shaped by the superstitious belief in the subject. And it is this superstition that makes us see everything on the basis of what to do and what to endure.[8] This perspective is formed following the will to find someone who is responsible, a will conditioned by the sentiment of fear, which in turn finds its justification in a reality where nature, not yet subdued by technique, shows itself as a permanent threat. This fear causes the institution of a complex metaphysical view of reality (by attributing causes) only by means of the complex mediations of the social realm. This is precisely what we see, for example, in *Twilight of the Idols*, in the concluding paragraphs of the section on the four great errors, where belief in causality is linked with belief in responsibility, and this leads to the "priests placed at the top of the ancient communities" who wanted to find at all costs those who were responsible in order to impose and inflict penalties, that is, in order to exercise one of the most basic aspects of power.

The "produced" aspect of the subject harks then back to a series of acts of metaphorization and interpretation that are determined by the social relations of power. These relations, however, do not falsify or distort anything: rather, they *posit* (*pongono*) the world of things, of causality, of the subject-object relation. As it is given to us today, this world does indeed have a history, however, and it is the one provisionally sealed off by the death of God, in other words, by the realization that when it comes to subject, responsibility, or causes, "we do not believe a word of it." From this perspective, however, we are not compelled to turn to less superficial, truer and originary structures—the very notion of force is only a *Bezeichnung*, a characterization by means of a sign, that is to say, a play on words and a linguistic effect, again much like the subject.[9]

The reasons for excluding the possibility of calling the Nietzschean *Übermensch* a subject are lodged within the destitution of the notion of subject as a notion tied to morality and Platonic-Christian metaphysics. We have, therefore, a better reason yet not to call the *Übermensch* a reconciled subject. (It would not be difficult to show, even in detail, that the notion of reconciliation is closely knit with that of subject; insofar as reconciliation is the removal of a conflict, it entails also a substantial conservation, the conservation of a substrate . . . a *subjectum*, to be precise.) This, however, does not mean that the notion of *Übermensch*—much like other late Nietzschean *Leitworte* connected to it, such as eternal recurrence, will to power, nihilism—is an untranslated, *nonmetaphorical* notion, a word endowed with its own "ownmost" sense, in other words, an essence that somehow falls outside the general law of interpretation, metaphorization, translation. Quite the contrary, it is precisely the theoretical status of Nietzsche's philosophical *Leitworte* to furnish us the key to understand the sense of the prefix *über* in the term *Übermensch*, as well as and more broadly the non-dialectical character of its overcoming of the Western metaphysical tradition.

The surfacing of the metaphorical, produced, character of metaphysical notions such as thing and object does not lead to the recovery of more fundamental structures of production, but to the overt generalization of production itself. It is this, I think, that makes for Nietzsche's peculiar position with respect to the philosophical tradition, and for the radically ultra-metaphysical character of his thought. Affirmations such as the one we cited above, according to which what happened in the meantime is that we no longer believe in the dogmas of metaphysics, or we believe in the thesis of the *Gay Science* whereby "God is dead," which is not a poetic way of saying that God does not exist but rather the strong acknowledgement of an event that has occurred—these affirmations disclose one of the fundamental mechanisms of Nietzsche's thought: the idea that the emerging of the nihilistic essence of becoming is an event that derives from the very logic of the development of metaphysics; and moreover, that becoming aware of this represents a real change in the history of metaphysics itself (but not because we thus recover the true essence of being against false and alienated theories). What happens, rather, is what I think we can call an obvious generalizing, and intensifying, of metaphoric production itself. This is basically what we find described in the most pointed manner in the ample fragment on European nihilism from the summer of 1887.[10] Or even in the long paragraph 9 of the third section of *On the Genealogy of Morals* ("What Is the Meaning of Ascetic Ideals?"), where we read of the condition of the human being who has come to understand the erroneous traits of the ascetic ideals and in general of the metaphysical view of the world. The condition of this person, who is the modern human being insofar as such an individual comes to terms with the death of God, is not the condition of the one who might have finally found peace in the acknowledgement of truth. Rather, this condition is marked by hubris, a sort of violence against oneself and things:

> Our whole attitude toward nature, the ways in which we violate her with the aid of machines and the heedless inventiveness of our technicians and engineers, is *hubris* . . . our attitude toward *ourselves* is *hubris*, for we experiment with ourselves in a way we would never permit ourselves to experiment with animals.[11]

Though there is no documentable etymological link here, nevertheless I think that the most illuminating reference for understanding Nietzsche's *über* is precisely the notion of hubris as theorized in these pages from *On the Genealogy of Morals*. What constitutes the passage to the overhuman condition, as well as what constitutes the passage from passive nihilism to active nihilism, is not therefore the establishment of a condition of spiritual wellbeing, clarity, reconciliation, and end of conflicts but, rather, a freeing of the forces at play, an intensifying of the whole vital sphere which consists, as Nietzsche writes in *Beyond Good and Evil*, in "estimating, preferring, being unjust, being limited, wanting to be different."[12]

Is the ideal of a humanity reconciled through possession of truth and the explicit assumption of reason as the guide for historical existence here contrasted with a vitalist vindication of biological forces, of the struggle for life and for domination? Or better said: Are we thus opposing, against the humanistic-metaphysical tradition (which was most recently expressed in the belief in the dialectical unfolding of history), the reduction of existence to the hubris of the manifold technical procedures of control and organization of reality (as Heidegger holds when he considers Nietzsche, precisely in this perspective, as the philosopher of the conclusion-triumph of metaphysics, which has now turned entirely into scientific organization of the world)?

In both these interpretations of Nietzsche, and especially in the first one, we are witness to the individuation of a "force" called "vital force" (or impulse of conservation and expansion) in the first case, while in the second it appears as force of technical rationality effectively ordering the world (force which, as Heidegger says, can in no way be mistaken for vitalism as celebration of the murky swirl of the biological). Against both interpretations, however, I suggest we take seriously those texts of Nietzsche's in which he excludes that force can in any way be named and identified, and transforms it instead into a fundamentally hermeneutic fact. The discovery of the senselessness (*insensatezza*) of becoming which takes place with the unfolding of nihilism is also, and inextricably, an affirmation of hubris. But this hubris, though, precisely because it arises as the recognition of the hermeneutic character of all alleged facts—there are no facts, only interpretations—cannot but give itself as interpretation *in progress*. Contrary to what may appear at first, then, we do not want to suggest a fleshed out version of Nietzsche's exaltation of force and power; rather, we want to think to its ultimate consequences the sense of the dissolution undergone by the notion of thing in itself to the benefit of the affirmation of the interpretative structure of being. In such a structure—which is so named only as a metaphysical metaphor, since it is nothing that can be fixed and recognized as a datum; rather, it is the result of a "hybrid" affirmation, of an interpretive act—in such a structure, there is no room for a reconciled subject in which the attained identity of sense and event means also the fulfilment and conclusion of the dialectical movement. *Übermensch* should therefore be translated, more than with "overman" (*oltreuomo*), with "man of the beyond" (*uomo dell'oltre*), conferring to the prefix an adjectival function. What characterizes the *Übermensch* as his most proper attribute is the act of overcoming (*oltrepassamento*) as an exercise of hubris. But if we take seriously that dissolution of the thing in itself which Nietzsche meant to produce with his own very work, then hubris cannot be understood other than in a hermeneutic sense.

The *über* of the Nietzschean *Übermensch*, therefore, does not allude to an overcoming of a dialectical kind, nor does it hark to the exercise of the will to life which is manifested in the struggle for existence or, less grossly, in the scientific-technological programming (*pianificazione*) of the world. The *über* is thought instead on the basis of the characteristic structure of the hermeneutic experience. This experience is conceived by Nietzsche in a way that is radically anti-metaphysical, not as access to being through the removal of the masks that being has adopted or were imposed on it, but as a tried and true event of being (*accadere dell'essere*) (and ultimately, as an expansion of being). It is such an ultra-metaphysical vision of hermeneutics that Nietzsche attempts to define by means of the notions of force and will to power. In fact, traits of hubris belong to interpretation as such, insofar as "forcing, adjusting, abbreviating, omitting, padding, inventing, falsifying" are constitutive of all interpretation.[13] All this obtains precisely because interpretation cannot be metaphysically legitimated as the grasping of the essence proper to a thing. Whereas the notion of hegemony (which entails an idea of sovereignty as understood by Gramsci, the idea of a deep correspondence between master and subject) can be considered typical of a metaphysical-dialectical vision, Nietzsche's insistence on force and on hubris excludes precisely this reconciled ideal of sovereignty as hegemony. Interpretation is constitutively injustice, superimposition, violence. The *Übermensch* exercises hubris with full awareness, whereas the traditional human being has always refused out of choice but more often through the masks imposed by the logic of social domination, to recognize this fact, developing as a result into a wretched being, a neurotic coward. The history of culture manifests an interpretative, hybrid structure, but this is also what for Nietzsche constitutes its permanent value. The history of the previous periods of humanity is not to be refused as history of violence, of the bloody "mnemotechnique" through which human beings became capable of living in a society and of organizing social work on the basis of rational schemes. What has become recognizable specifically through this mnemotechnique is the violence implicit in all interpretative processes. Yet, once it is recognized explicitly as constitutive of the givenness of things, violence changes meaning also: it becomes, much like all metaphysical terms (cause, principle, substance, subject, etc.), an explicitly hermeneutic term. The names it took on in the past (that is, the names of metaphysical entities), as well as the very name of force, are given explicitly as fictions (*finzioni*)—the true world, or the metaphysical *ontos on*, has become a fable, as Nietzsche writes in *Twilight of the*

Idols. God is dead, now we want the *Übermensch* to live. The overman however can only live as the human being of the *über*, or also, according to the beautiful image in *The Gay Science*, as the human being who knows how to continue to dream aware that he or she is dreaming.[14] Not as a reconciled subject because there is no identity between *appearing* and *being*. The Nietzschean subject is appearance *only*, and is no longer defined in relation to being. The term indicates solely that the self-giving of something as something is a perspective, violently superimposing itself on other perspectives which, only on the basis of an inner exigency of interpretation, are identified with the thing itself. In Nietzsche's thesis, according to which the will to power means conferring to becoming the traits of being, the emphasis should be placed on becoming, and not on being.[15] For it is not a question of finally attributing to becoming, also, the strong traits of being, but, rather, it is to becoming that one must give—with everything that this entails—the attributes that earlier belonged to being. On this we shall return in order to assess the ontological implications of Nietzsche's hermeneutics. Within the discourse on *Übermensch* and subject, this means that everything that is disclosed as being is actually becoming, and that is, interpretative production. As the bringing out of the constitutive *hubris* of all experience, of the universality of appearance and the impossibility of an identity between being and appearing, Nietzsche's doctrine of the *Übermensch* is here given in its most theoretically relevant light, and that is, as the extreme development and liquidation of any philosophy of reflection (*filosofia della riflessione*). With everything such a closing out implies, for example, in terms of the dissolution of the notion of *Bildung*.

As it turns out, the reference to *Bildung*, or to the idea of the formation of the individual which, within idealist historicism, attains crucial importance as the itinerary of the rise from empirical consciousness to transcendental consciousness, to the self-transparency of absolute spirit, this reference is no mere marginal note to the consequences of Nietzsche's dissolution of the notion of subject. Nietzsche's never ending effort to define through the *Wille zur Macht* the avenues for an explicitly planned and programmed breeding (*allevamento*) of the *Übermensch* is not only an "application" aspect of his philosophy, but is essential to the very definition of the contents of this thought.

The formation of the *Übermensch* as the individual characterized by hubris cannot be configured as hermeneutic process in the sense of the unmasking of the true essence of the human being and of being. However, it does contain this process as one of its inseparable aspects and moments. The object of the unmasking, in Nietzsche's writings—*Human, All Too Human; Dawn; The Gay Science*—is not some true ground (*fondo*) of things, but the interpretative process itself. The result of the unmasking, therefore, cannot be an appropriation of the true, but an explication of the production of lies. Zarathustra's most constant character trait is in fact that of being, at one and the same time, a solution finder and a creator of enigmas. Hubris is not only that which interpretation discovers behind the dogmas and values of metaphysical morality; it is also the very activity of this discovering. The values that have been handed down are not dismissed as apparent; rather, they are merely overcome through acts of superimposition, further falsification, injustice. In such a way, though, the reconciliation that was denied to the *Übermensch* insofar as impossible reconciliation between being and appearing seems to return as absolutization of appearance. But now, will not the hubris of the *Übermensch* be in fact the pure explosion of a free metaphorizing activity, the spreading about of the creativity of symbols, enigmas, metaphors, which would thus become, despite everything, the recovery of an authentic humanity freed from the limitations that metaphysics and morality have imposed on it? Reading Nietzsche along these lines finds broad support in contemporary culture, especially within French thought. Undue oversimplifications often occur, however, when one tries to identify a "desiring" current within such culture somehow connected to Nietzsche, as, for instance, in Deleuze's overly schematic theses. Beyond schematizations, though, it remains true that Deleuze's theoretical proposal—in *Difference and Repetition*, for example—entails a "glorification of the simulacrum" that falls neatly in line with the absolutization of appearance, which in its turn rests on the attribution to becoming of the strong, affirmative, imposing traits of being. Deleuze's position however does not entail taking up becoming as the sole unique being, which would thus find itself divested precisely of its metaphysical and in some way disempowered (*depotenziate*) connotations.

What lies hidden here is an extremely metaphysical misunderstanding (*equivoco*) in reading Nietzsche, which is doubly metaphysical, first, because it still entails the identification of *force*, to which a name is conferred, namely, creativity and symbolic freedom opposed to social limitation, imposition of codes, etc.; and second, because in this identifying of force we find overlaid—albeit as attributed to the simulacra—the luminous, affirmative characters that have always belonged to metaphysical being.

Such a misunderstanding is countered by what we may label the *experimental conception* of the *Übermensch*. In the perspective of an over-humanness as emancipation of a limitless creative activity, what cannot be explained is the fact that the overman exercises *hubris* above all on himself: "We perform experiments on ourselves which we would never think of performing on animals" writes Nietzsche in *On the Genealogy of Morals*. The subject has no authentic constitution to emancipate, and this not even in the sense of a vital activity that one should set free, of impulses or desires that might be found beyond the removal or repression that would constitute culture. Nietzsche's nominalism is total. The subject is nothing else than the activity of positing, overcoming, falsifying (*porre, oltrepassare, falsificare*). Therefore, its impulses and desires too are the products of positions and falsifications. The experiment does not consist in the act by which one discovers that at the ground of metaphysical moral values there is a "human, all too human" reality, but in asking oneself, at the end of this process of unmasking, if and "whether science can furnish goals of actions after it has proved that it can take such goals away and annihilate them."[16] Nietzsche calls this experiment "heroism." However, to face this problem heroically means taking stock of the hermeneutic nature of being and of experience.

What remains indeterminate, in *The Gay Science*, is a crucial aspect of the experiment, and that is the criterion on the basis of which we can say whether it has succeeded or failed. Given that interpretation is an act of violence and superimposition, we cannot think of its success as measurable in terms of a greater or lesser correspondence with the essence of things. Essence is the name given to the result of the experiment, to the thing as it is constituted during the interpretative act. In the posthumously published 1873 writing *On Truth and Lying in an Extra-Moral Sense*, Nietzsche had dealt with this issue in terms which it is interesting to compare to the hermeneutics of his later texts. In the unpublished 1873 text, the experience of human beings in the world is described in terms of the production of metaphors—the emotive reactions stimulated by the encounter with things are associated to images and objects, become concepts and names for them, without there being between the ones and the others any objective link. The world of truth is constituted when, with the rise of organized society, a given metaphorical system is adopted as canonical and imposed on everyone (if one wants to communicate, that is, live within that society). There are also other metaphorical systems; however, they are confined to purely subjective validity, and constitute the sphere of poetry and of artistic production in general.

༄

Compared to this structure in Nietzsche's unpublished, youthful work, the later hermeneutic thesis represents a key turning point. The turn is given by the introduction of the notion of force. In the 1873 essay, Nietzsche does indeed hold fast to the metaphoric, that is to say, interpretative, hybrid, character of all knowing and also to the thesis that the establishment of an interpretation as truth is the fruit of an intervention external to the metaphorical activity, therefore the fruit of an act of force. But it remains a rigid scheme, which in fact is resolved (albeit not explicitly, given the fragmentary nature of the writing), through a sort of counter-foisting between a free poetic activity (felt as natural and proper to the state of nature), and the obligation to lie on the basis of precise rules. The Rousseauian aspects in this Nietzschean theory of language have been pointed out, for example, by Bernard Pautrat.[17] If followed to its ultimate consequence, while keeping it isolated from the developments and complications of Nietzsche's mature hermeneutics, the structure of the essay on truth and lying leads to a flattening of the idea of the *Übermensch* onto the idea of the freeing of an allegedly natural symbolic activity from any limit of a social-communicative character. The metaphorizing activity, the hermeneutic hubris, does indeed experience a process of emancipation when the true world becomes a fable, but this is in favor neither of the reestablishment of a hypothetical, idyllic state of nature, nor of a pure and simple introduction of chaos in social communication. It is true that the rigidity of the communicative codes, and of any kind of codes, has long been required by the exigencies of the organization of labor within a state strongly dependent on nature. This rigidity, today, can be slackened, and this is what takes place with the death of God and the fall of any metaphysical structure of the universe. But the social system turning elastic and metaphysics dropping out of sight do not necessarily entail the pure, untrammeled explosion of a symbolic activity bound by no limit or need for validation (*validazione*). The whole activity of perpetrating violence and falsifying which goes into interpretation is thought of as an experiment. And this requires a tried and true self-transcending on the part of the interpreter: Nietzsche in fact speaks of *Selbstverneinen, Sich-selbst-überwinden* (self-transcending).[18] The experiment is not, therefore, pure effusion, it requires an effort that somehow presupposes a normative criterion. Only in this way can we speak, as Nietzsche does, of experimenting above all with oneself.

When compared with the situation described in the essay on truth and lying, this notion of experiment is more attentive to the play of forces, putting out of range any Rousseauian reading of Nietzsche's philosophy. There is no metaphoric activity that escapes the play of forces, the impositions of codes. There is no symbolization at the state of nature. Both the metaphors and the subject therein expressed are constituted as always-already in a complex interpretative play. Introducing the notion of force in hermeneutics means not only underscoring the impositive, nominalist essence of interpretation, but also bringing into view its ever differential character. A force is never absolute, it is always measured and displayed against other forces. There is no struggle among supposedly ultimate subjects so that some could impose themselves on others; there is, instead, their coming into being as subjects within a play of forces which somehow precedes them. Nietzsche refers to this play when he speaks of how the *Übermensch* overcomes and negates himself in that experiment which is the very exercise of the hermeneutic hubris. If it is difficult to explicate exactly what this radical hermeneutic is, it is at least clear what it is not. It is not a doctrine of the will to domination (*dominio*), because the latter supposes in fact that the struggle takes place among subjects understood as ultimate metaphysical points. The mechanisms for the constitution-destitution of the subject as outcome of a complex play of metaphors, of recognitions and adjustments of forces, are what Nietzsche tried to describe in the monumental preparatory work for the *Wille zur Macht*, which configures itself as the sketch for a hermeneutic ontology in the double sense of this term: a knowledge of being which begins with the unmasking reconstruction of the human all too human origins of the supreme values and objects of traditional metaphysics; and a theory of the conditions of possibility of a being which is given explicitly as the result of interpretative processes. "To continue to dream aware that we are dreaming," according to the expression from *The Gay Science* to which we hark continuously from any point in Nietzsche's thought.

Nietzsche's relative failure, the incompleteness of the projected *Hauptwerke*, which the *Wille zur Macht* was supposed to be, the very problematic character of the key notions of his late philosophy, and the difficulty of ordering them in an all-coherent whole—all of this coincides simply with the difficulties confronting any contemporary project of a hermeneutic ontology. However, the study of the meaning of Nietzsche's *Übermensch* should allow us at least to clarify a few points, on which we think we can build further.

1. First of all, a radical hermeneutic ontology implies the abandonment of the metaphysical notion of subject understood as unity, even when this is thought of as the result of a dialectical process of identification. The normal condition of the *Übermensch* is scission. The philosophical sense of this Nietzschean view consists entirely in its placing itself at the extreme opposite of any philosophy of reflection as recomposition of the subject with itself, as *Bildung* in the sense this term has in modern culture. The philosophy of reflection captures indeed the divided character of the I, but at least in the dominant trend of nineteenth-century idealism, it exorcises it through the dialectic of self-identification.

The discovery of the constitutively split character of the subject links Nietzsche's thought to various aspects of twentieth-century culture, which find in this connection a unifying feature. On the one hand, the split subject, the Nietzschean overman is certainly the "I" experienced by avant-garde art and culture (not only in its most emblematic manifestations such as expressionism, but also in more classical figures such as Musil. Musil in fact takes from Nietzsche precisely those aspects that allude to dissolution, in statements such as *"Das Leben wohnt nicht mehr im Ganzen."*[19] And yet, on the other hand, next to this more dramatic vision of the constitutive split of the *Übermensch*, we cannot forget another sense of the concept, which has unfortunately been left in the shadow by Nietzsche scholarship and which contains, to my way of seeing it, the greatest potential for development. It is the aspect of the question that Nietzsche develops especially in the works of the middle period of his production, in *Human, All Too Human*, in *Daybreak*, and in *The Gay Science*. The split *Übermensch* is also, and above all, the individual of "good character" mentioned in a page from *Human, All Too Human*, that is, the individual who has relinquished all metaphysical certainties without reactive nostalgias, and is capable of appreciating the multiplicity of appearances as such. This overman is the human being that belongs to the world of intensified communication, or better yet, of metacommunication. I am thinking for example of the developments which hermeneutics has undergone through Habermas's recent work, with his theory of communicative competence, or, on a different ground, of the elaboration of a theory of games and fantasy as metacommunicative facts in the work of Gregory Bateson. The overhuman condition of the split subject does not configure itself solely as the experimental tension of the artistic, twentieth-century, avant-garde human being, but also and above all, I believe, as the normal condition of postmodern human beings in a world in which the intensification of communication—freed at both the political and the technical level—paves the road to an effective experience of individuality as multiplicity—to the dreaming knowing one is dreaming of which we read in *The Gay Science*.

2. Nietzsche's hermeneutic ontology is not only an anthropological doctrine, but also a theory of being that lists among its principles that of "attributing *to becoming* the character of being." As the critics who underscore the ultimately nihilistic traits of Nietzsche's thought can well perceive, the power which the will wants is possible only if this will has before itself being identified with nothingness. I would rather say instead that in order for the will—that is, the interpretative hubris—to be itself, it needs that being be weak. This alone makes possible that play of communication and metacommunication in which things are constituted and, together, also always deconstituted. As is the case for the overman, for the will to power too we need an interpretative commitment capable of eliminating all metaphysical misunderstandings. Even after the end of metaphysics, being remains still modelled upon the subject. But to the split subject that is the overman there can no longer correspond a being (*essere*) conceived with the traits—of power, force, definiteness, eternity, unfolded actuality—that tradition has always attributed to it. In the end, the theory of the will to power seems to lay the foundations for an ontology that repudiates precisely those elements of power which have dominated Western thinking and is actually pointed toward a weak conception of being. Thought in the light of a notion of the *Übermensch* as a hermeneutic-communicative fact, a weakened notion of being presents itself as the ontology adequate unexpectedly to account for some problematical aspects of human experience in the world of late modernity.

2

Towards an Ontology of Decline

According to a well-known Heideggerian *topos*, the name West (*Occidente*), *Abendland*, not only designates the site of our civilization on the geographic level, but denominates it also ontologically, insofar as the *Abendland* is the land of the twilight, of the setting of being (*tramonto dell'essere*). We can speak of an ontology of decline and see its preparation and its first elements in Heidegger's texts only if we interpret Heidegger's thesis on the West by changing its formulation to read not "The West is the land of the setting (of being)," but "The West is the land of the setting (and, therefore, of being)." As a matter of fact, another crucial Heideggerian formulation, which doubles as the title for a chapter in his *Nietzsche*, "Metaphysics as the History of Being,"[1] can also be read in the same way, provided we stress it properly, that is, in the only way that is in accordance with Heidegger's thought as a whole. Therefore, we do not read "metaphysics is the history of being" but rather "metaphysics is *the* history of being." This means that beyond metaphysics, there is no other history of being. Thus, the West is not that land where being sets, whereas elsewhere it shines (used to shine, will shine again) high in the noontime sky. The West is the land of being precisely insofar as it is also, inextricably, the land of the setting of being.

This reformulation of Heidegger's statement on the West entails taking a different position with respect to the more widely known interpretations of the meaning of his philosophy. The latter in fact can be generally thought of as emphasizing, alternatively, either the term "setting" or the term "being," at the expense of what I consider the indissoluble connection between the two. The term "being" is privileged by those interpretations that persist in reading Heidegger as the thinker who—though in a somewhat problematic and purely preparatory fashion—foresees a return of being, or to being, on the basis of a broadly defined religious perspective (better yet, a theological view, in the sense of the ontotheology addressed in *Identität und Differenz*).[2] The term "setting" is instead privileged by those interpretations that read Heidegger's thought as the invitation to take stock (*prendere atto*) of the fact that metaphysics is over, and with it any possible history of being. "There is nothing more" about being (*dell'essere "non ne è più nulla"*), in a total way; this excludes any mythical waiting for its possible novel addressing itself to us. Above and beyond their specific inner differences, the two camps have vigorously squared off to tally up their results. This can be read as a sign that perhaps the two elements that each camp isolates are indeed present and problematically linked in Heidegger's text. Our formulation intends to speak precisely to the connection between the two terms. Even upon a cursory reading, the formulation begins to account in an unimposing manner for what has always been considered an ambiguity on Heidegger's part *vis-à-vis* the history of metaphysics. Such ambiguity could be removed only if we were to interpret this history as the dialectical preparation for its own overcoming in the direction of a recalling thinking (*pensiero rammemorante*) such as the one Heidegger is trying to enact. However, *Metaphysik* as *Geschichte des Seins* is not a dialectical unfolding. The respect, the attention, better yet, the *pietas* which Heidegger manifests toward the history of that thought (in which, ever so evidently, there is nothing more about being) does not bear the dialectical justification of the identification of the real (that which occurs) with the rational. This *pietas* can instead be best explained by acknowledging that metaphysics is the destiny of being also and above all in the sense that it behooves being to set (*che all'essere "conviene" il tramontare*).

This also implies, however, that we can find in Heidegger's text the premises and the elements for a possible positive conception of being and not only the description of a condition of absence. Such a condition of absence could only be defined in relation (a relation of nostalgia, of waiting or even of liquidation as for instance in the case of the disavowal of metaphysics as myth or ideology) to the presence of being and its traditionally strong attributes according to Western metaphysics. These attributes are strong in more than a metaphoric sense, because beyond the verbal proximity there exists a close relation between the *enérgheia*, the actuality which characterizes Aristotle's being, and the *enárgheia*, the evidence, luminosity, vividness of what appears and imposes itself as true. Furthermore, there is a close relation between actuality and energy, and between the latter and real force. When Nietzsche speaks of metaphysics as an attempt to master reality through force, he is not describing a marginal trait of metaphysics.[3] He is describing its essence such as it manifests itself already in the first pages of Aristotle's *Metaphysics*, where knowledge is defined in relation to the possession of first principles.

I believe that interpreters and followers of Heidegger have failed to develop as little as the first basic elements of an ontology of decline (*ontologia del declino*). Exception can be made, perhaps, for Gadamer's hermeneutics with his well-known thesis according to which "being that can be understood is language."[4] And yet, even in this formulation, the relation language-being is studied almost always from the standpoint of language, and not from the side of the consequences it may have on ontology itself. For example, in Gadamer, Heidegger's notion of metaphysics is hardly developed at all. The lack of a theoretical elaboration of the ontology of decline among Heidegger followers may depend on the fact that, any contrary *Warnung* notwithstanding, Heidegger's meditation on being is still thought of in terms of foundation. Heidegger, however, had instead called attention to the necessity of "letting go of being as foundation (*lasciare perdere l'essere come fondamento*)"[5] if we wish to start on our way toward recalling thinking (*pensiero rammemorante*). Unless I am mistaken, Heidegger spoke of *Fundamentalontologie* (*Fundamental Ontology*) only in *Sein und Zeit* (*Being and Time*), whereas his other texts make repeated mention of *Begründung* (justification); this is always with reference to metaphysics though, which is precisely that thought which moves in the horizon where a *Grund* (reason) is conferred. Nevertheless, we cannot deny that in *Sein und Zeit* there is an attempt at establishing a foundation, at least in the broad sense of the word. The question addressed there was in fact that of the sense of being, that is, the horizon within which alone an entity (*ente*) gives itself as something. Yet right from the beginning, through the relevance given to the epigraph passage from the *Sophist* which opens the work, the research is immediately oriented toward a historical condition. There is no instance where the research is turned toward the pure conditions of possibility—of the phenomenon, of knowledge—in the Kantian sense. If we are allowed a pun, we are faced with a situation in which Kant's condition of possibility is revealed as inescapably connected with a condition understood as the status of things. Such a connection is the authentic theme of discourse.

In *Sein und Zeit*, we are not looking for and do not find the transcendental conditions of possibility for the experience of beings (*ente*). Rather, we perceive in a meditating manner those conditions under which alone, as it turns out, our experience of beings can be given. Obviously this does not mean totally abandoning the transcendental plane, the interest in individuating the conditions of possibility in the Kantian sense. But the research must come to terms from the very beginning with the fact that it can only be carried out within inextricable connections with the individuation of conditions in the factual sense of the term. This is a point upon which it pays to insist, especially in relation to some recent returns, even within the hermeneutic camp (I am thinking of Apel and Habermas), to broadly Kantian orientations. Yet one of the elements which, already in *Sein und Zeit*, constitutes the basis for an ontology of decline is precisely the specific physiognomy assumed by "foundation." For, precisely because of the radical way in which in that work the question of being is posited—with the immediate shift to the analytic of existence—it is clear that any possible answer to the question can no longer, at least in theory, configure itself as foundation, not only in the sense of the conferring of a *Grund*, of the principle of sufficient reason, but also and more broadly in the sense that thinking can no longer expect to attain a position from which it can avail itself, in whatever way, of the being (*ente*) which should be founded. Already in *Sein und Zeit*, being is "let go as foundation." Instead of being as capable of functioning as *Grund*, what we glimpse—especially with regard to the centrality of the existential analytic and the elucidation of the nexus with time—is "Being as constitutively no longer capable of founding anything: therefore being as weak and disempowered (*un essere debole e depotenziato*). The sense of being which *Sein und Zeit* searches for and to some degree attains is to be understood above all as a direction in which *Dasein* and being find themselves already pointed, in a movement that leads them not to a stable base, but to a further and permanent dislocation wherein they are dispossessed and deprived of any center. The situation described by Nietzsche (in a note which opened the old edition of *Der Wille zur Macht*) as characteristic of nihilism, namely, that beginning with Copernicus "man rolls away from the center toward an X," is also that of Heidegger's *Dasein*. Much like the post-Copernican human being, *Dasein* is not the founding center, nor does it inhabit, possess, or coincide with this center. In the radical unfolding which it has in *Sein und Zeit*, the search for the sense of being shows progressively that this sense is given to human beings only as direction toward dispossession and degrounding (*spossessamento e sfondamento*).

Therefore, even against Heidegger's texts, we must say that the search begun in *Sein und Zeit* does not lead us toward the overcoming of nihilism, but rather toward the experience of nihilism as the sole possible path for ontology. This thesis clashes against the letter of Heidegger's texts because in them nihilism means the flattening of being on beings, that is, the forgetting of being which characterizes Western metaphysics, and which in the end reduces being to a value (in Nietzsche), that is, to a validity posited and recognized by and for the subject. And so it turns out that nothing is left of being as such. This is not the place to discuss whether and how nihilism thus understood is entirely faithful to Nietzsche's position. Yet it should be clear that, especially through his use of the notion of nihilism to indicate the fulfilling of the forgetting of being in the final moment of metaphysics, Heidegger himself contributed to the expectation that from his thought—insofar as it is alternative to or at least an attempt at overcoming—we could recover being in its foundational force and function: which is the contrary of what happens in nihilism. Instead, what is suggested here is that it is precisely this foundational force and function which still partake of the horizon of nihilism: being as *Grund* is only an earlier moment in the linear development which leads to being as value. This of course is well known to all readers of Heidegger; yet we ought to continue to think about this in order to draw the (relevant) consequences. The peculiar connection between foundation and degrounding which takes place in *Sein und Zeit* ultimately means that the search for the sense of being cannot give rise to the attainment of a strong position, but only to the assumption of nihilism as a movement on the basis of which the human being, *Dasein*, rolls away from the center toward the X.

The nexus founding-degrounding runs through the entirety of *Sein und Zeit* and emerges in particular places, for instance, with the inclusion of *Befindlichkeit*, affectivity (*la situazione emotiva*), among the existentials, that is, among the constitutive modes of the disclosure of *Dasein*, those which in Heidegger to all effects replaces Kantian transcendentals. Or in those moments like the description of the hermeneutic circle, in light of which truth appears as bound to interpretation as the elaboration of the pre-comprehension in which being-there is always-already thrown for the mere fact of existing. The nexus is especially visible in the constitutive function which being-towards-death exercises with respect to the historicity of *being-there*.

∽

The function and relevance of being-towards-death is a core theme from *Sein und Zeit* that has most resisted further interpretation and theoretical elaboration (authoritative interpreters such as Gadamer, for example, even question its connection to the whole of Heidegger's thought). The discourse on being-towards-death is exemplary (even at the structural level) of the way in which *Sein und Zeit*, starting out in search of a foundation still somehow metaphysical, ends up with nihilistic outcomes, at least in the sense I have alluded to. Heidegger comes upon being-towards death, in fact,[6] by raising a problem which at first sight is eminently metaphysical, both in form and content. Does the existential analytic developed in the first part of the work give us *Dasein* in the totality of its structures? But, Heidegger seems to ask himself immediately after, what does being a totality mean for *Dasein*? Coherently pursued, this problem leads one to perceive that being-there constitutes itself as a totality, and therefore "founds" itself,[7] to the degree in which it anticipates its own death (because the assignation of *Grund*, which constitutes the foundation, always means closure in the series of connections, that is, the constitution of a totality, as opposed to infinite regress). Freely translating Heidegger's language, we can say: being-there is really *there* (l'esserci *ci* è davvero), that is, it distinguishes itself from other intrawordly beings (*enti*) insofar as it constitutes itself as a historical totality, which passes continuously, that is historically, through the various possibilities that slowly and by degrees, whether becoming real or disappearing, do make up its existence. Even inauthentic existing, insofar as it is a simply defective mode of historical existence as continuity, is related to being-towards-death—its constitutive category is still and always dying, though experienced in the form of *das Man*, in the everyday sense that "one dies." The constitution of being-there in a historical continuum is radically related to death inasmuch as the latter—as the permanent possibility of the impossibility of all other possibilities, and therefore as authentic possibility insofar as possibility that is authentic (*possibilità autentica in quanto autentica possibilità*)—allows all other possibilities to be on this side of it, so to speak, preventing them from congealing in exclusive possibility-reality, yet allowing instead that they constitute themselves as a tissue-text.

All this, however, means that being-there exists and therefore serves as site for the illumination of the truth of being (that is, of the drawing of entities to being) only insofar as it is constituted as the possibility of not-being-there-any longer (*non-esserci-più*). Heidegger insists often on the fact that this relation with death ought not be read in a purely *ontic* way, and therefore not even in a biological sense. At any rate, as in all moments in which philosophy encounters similar passage points (above all, that between culture and nature), this Heideggerian distinction too is mired in ambiguity. If in fact it is true that being-there is historical—that is, it exists as continued *discursus* endowed with possible senses—only insofar as it can die and explicitly anticipates its own death, it is also true that it is historical in the sense of being able to avail itself of determinate and qualified possibilities, having relation with past and future generations precisely because it is born and dies in the literal, biological sense of the term. The historicity of being-there is not only the constitution of existence as tissue-text, it is also the belonging to an epoch, the *Geworfernheit* (thrownness), which, after all, intimately qualifies the project within which being-there and beings relate to one another, come to being in ways marked differently each and every time. This double meaning of historicity in its relation to being-towards-death is one locus where the nexus founding-degrounding is more explicitly, albeit problematically, manifested—a nexus representing one of the senses, and I would venture perhaps *the* sense, of *Sein und Zeit*.

If and to what degree explicating this nexus entails also renewed attention not only to the ontological, but also to the *ontic* and biologic meaning of death is a question to be taken up elsewhere. What we are interested in showing here is that the being-towards of which Heidegger speaks can no longer be thought in metaphysical terms; not even when it is qualified as *hidden* or *absent*. It is therefore false and deceiving to think that Heidegger's ontology is a theory of being as force and obscured luminosity (obscured by some catastrophic event or even by an inner limitation of being itself, its epochality) and that it wants to prepare the path for the return of being, understood once again as luminosity and founding force. Only if we persist in thinking along these lines can we then be shocked by the thesis according to which the *outcome of Heidegger's meditation, beginning already with* Sein und Zeit, *is the assumption of nihilism*. In the degrounding sense experienced also by Nietzsche in the cited note from *Der Wille zur Macht*, nihilism is a present but not dominant thread in the metaphysical tradition, which has always rather preferred to move along the lines of the logic of *Grund*, of substance and value. Though we are here but at the beginning, to recognize thoroughly the implications of this Heideggerian nihilism means, for example, locking out those interpretations of his thought in terms more or less implicit of negative theology—whether these latter understand him as the theoretician of the *dürftige Zeit* (meagre times) who regrets and waits for the strong presence of being (as presence of a transcendent being, for example, or even as decisive historical event, which opens a new history for the no-longer alienated human being). Or whether they understand his announcement of the end of metaphysics as freeing the field for an experience organized in a wholly independent manner from being (characterized yet again as a metaphysical imposition).

On the basis of the interpretation submitted in these pages, the outcome (*esito*) of Heidegger's thought is not the realization that the guaranteed foundation of metaphysical being cannot (any longer or yet) be given, and that as a result thinking must either regret its not being there or else prepare to usher it in again. Nor is it an outcome of Heidegger's thought the becoming aware (*prender atto*) that such a foundation is finally rendered in vain. Therefore, we can and should proceed to the construction of a non-ontological humanity, devoted exclusively to beings (*enti*), committed to the techniques of organization and planning of their diverse fields. Besides, this latter position, lacking (much like the first one) a critique of the "strong" conception of being, finds itself precisely with this conception in its hands without recognizing it, insofar as it ends up attributing to beings (*enti*) and their environments the same peremptory authoritativeness which thought in the past attributed to metaphysical being.

∽

As if in a sort of therapeutic exercise, we must therefore continually rethink the nexus founding-degrounding that is announced in *Sein und*

Zeit and runs through the entire subsequent development in Heidegger's works. Not only does it emerge in the ambiguity of being-towards-death, but it also alludes to a non-transcendental (and therefore also metaphysically not-strong) relation between fact and right, which discloses a totally new conception of the very notion of foundation. Although *Sein und Zeit* started on the search for the sense of being as if it concerned the individuation of a transcendental condition of possibility of our experience, immediately the condition of possibility revealed itself to be also the historical-finite condition of *Dasein*, which is indeed project (therefore a sort of transcendental screen), but a thrown project (conditioned time and again by diverse pre-comprehensions, which are co-originarily rooted in the emotive situation, or *Befindlichkeit* (sensitivities). In this way the foundation is not attained, at most it takes shape (*si delinea*) since it is not something like a still point we can reach and therefore stop. This foundation can only be called, with an oxymoron, *hermeneutic foundation*. Because it works by founding only (mostly) in this sense, being (*l'essere*) is charged with a connotation that is totally alien to the metaphysical tradition, and which corresponds to what we mean with the formulation "*ontology of decline*" ("*ontologia del declino*").

Before Heidegger, the idea of a hermeneutic foundation is to be found in Nietzsche, and not by chance, we might add, since both thinkers move within the horizon of nihilism. Let us read as an example the beautiful aphorism 82 from *The Wanderer and His Shadow*, titled "Affected Salutations":

> If you want to free yourself from a party or a religion, you think it is necessary to confute them. But this is a lofty ideal. What is necessary is only that you clearly comprehend what hooks kept you tied to this party or this religion, and that now are unhooked; and what motivations drove you this or that way. We did not take up arms for this or that party or religion *just for the sake of knowing them*; but neither should we *affect* this when we bid them farewell.

Is this solely a reference to the "human, all too human" roots of everything we consider validity and value? It may be so. But the sense of this aphorism can be grasped in its entirety only if we relate it to the announcement that "God is dead," a proclamation which is at once the truth which founds the thought of degrounding (*pensiero dello sfondamento*) (there is no longer a strong metaphysical structure of being), and the recognition that this "truth" cannot but be, peculiarly, a matter of fact (*constatazione di fatto*). To read this hermeneutic foundation as if it amounted to a profession of historicist faith would be mistaken, for it would mean that we are still within the horizon of the metaphysical meaning of being: but a being that with its presence ever elsewhere, or even with its pure and simple absence, simply continues to devaluate everything which is not founded in the strong sense, making it thus drop into the domain of appearance, of what is relative, of non-value. However, *Dasein*'s finite-historical thrownness never allows for an upturning of the existential analytic onto the plane of the individuation of banal-historical details pertaining to epochs and societies, insofar as to radicalize the historicity of the thrown project leads precisely to questioning the claims of a historicist foundation. Moreover, it leads to reopening the problem of whether historical epochs and humanity are possible at the level of the *Geschick* of being. Radicalizing the historicity of the thrown project and positing the problem at the level of the *Geschick* (destiny) of being are precisely what happens with the turn, the *Kehre* (turn) in Heidegger's thinking beginning in the early thirties. Yet the *Kehre* will not be reduced to a more or less secretive rehashing of historicism if only we clearly recognize in it the procedure of the hermeneutic foundation, which requires as one of its corollaries the explicit enunciation of an ontology of decline. The sense of the *Kehre* is the coming to light of the fact that thinking means founding, but that founding can only have a hermeneutic sense. After the *Kehre*, Heidegger incessantly retraces the pathways of the history of metaphysics, making use of that arbitrary tool par excellence (at least from the viewpoint of the exigencies of the foundational rigor of metaphysics) which is etymology. After all, everything we know about hermeneutic foundation is right here. Entities (*enti*) consign themselves to being-there within the horizon of a project which is not the transcendental constitution of Kant's reason, but the finite-historical thrownness that unfolds between birth and death and within the limits of an epoch, a language, a society. The "who throws" of the thrown project, at any rate, is neither life understood biologically, nor society or language or culture. It is, says Heidegger, being itself (l'essere stesso). Being has its paradoxical positivity precisely in not being any of these supposed foundational horizons, and in setting them rather in a state of indefinite oscillation. As a thrown project, *Dasein* rolls away from the center toward the X. The horizons within which beings (*enti*) (including *Dasein* itself) appear to *Dasein* are horizons which have roots in the past and are open toward the future, in short, they are historical-finite horizons. To identify them does not mean having them at one's disposal, but rather refers to ulterior connections, as in the etymological reconstruction of words which make up our language.

This hermeneutic retracing *in infinitum* is the sense of being that is sought in *Sein und Zeit*, but this sense of being is something entirely different from the notion of being that metaphysics has handed down to us. Before Heidegger, and Nietzsche, in the history of thought there is only one other decisive example of a theory of hermeneutic foundation, and that is Kant's deduction of the judgments of taste in the *Critique of Judgement*. Here once again, the foundation (in the specific case, the peculiar universality of the judgments on beauty) ends up being a reference to the co-belongingness of subject and humanity, a co-belonging that is problematic and constantly about to happen, as problematic and constantly about to happen is the humanity that shares the *sensus communis* sought by the judgment of taste.

I think that Heidegger's meditation on the essence of technology (*tecnica*) and on the notion of the *Ge-stell* (frame) is the most important document to turn to in order to begin to think of the hermeneutic foundation in more articulate terms. A thesis such as we find in *Identität und Differenz*, according to which "in the frame (*Ge-Stell*), we glimpse a first, oppressing flash of the appropriation (*Ereignis*),"[8] can be favorably compared, both in style and content, to Nietzsche's announcement of the death of God. As in Nietzsche's "God is dead," here also we are confronted with the announcement of a founding/degrounding event (*evento fondante-sfondante*): founding insofar as it defines and determines (in the sense in which *be-stimmt* suggests also tune-in) the conditions (the possibility, the fact) of the coming of beings to being (*del venire degli enti all'essere*); degrounding insofar as this condition is defined and determined precisely as deprived of any foundation in the metaphorical sense of the term.

As is well known, *Ge-stell* is the term employed by Heidegger to refer generally to modern technology (*la tecnica moderna*), to its *Wesen* in the contemporary world as an element which determines, *be-stimmt*, the horizon of *Dasein*. In Italian, we translate the term *Ge-stell* with "*im-posizione*" ("im-position"), with a hyphen, so as to emphasize both the originary *Stellen*, placing, and the sense of "setting in position" (*"messa in posizione"*) and of cogency which Heidegger attributes to it. What is lost, instead, is the sense of the *ge-* as a collective prefix, which indicates the whole of placing (though the cogency to which im-position alludes is perhaps also the most salient and fundamental characteristic of the sense of "whole" of technological ordering or positing (*del senso di "insieme" del porre tecnico*). As the whole of the technological world, the *Ge-stell* defines the condition (the situation) of our specific historical-finite thrownness. It is also the condition of possibility through which beings come to being in this specific epoch. But as with any condition of possibility, this one is not open only in the "descendant" sense, that is, it does not only make beings (*enti*) appear each for what it is (*als etwas*). It is also the flashing of the *Er-eignis*. This is another key-term in the thought of the later Heidegger; literally, it means "event" (*evento*), but is employed by Heidegger with explicit reference to the term *eigen* proper, ownmost (*proprio*), to which it is related. *Er-eignis* is thus the event in which each being (*ente*) is "propriated, owned (*propriato*)," and thus appears as that which it is insofar as it is also and inseparably implied in a movement of trans-propriation. Even before things, the movement of trans-propriation concerns human beings and being. In the *Er-eignis* in which beings come to being, it happens that the human being is *ver-eignet* (appropriated) to being, and being is *zugeeignet* (handed over, delivered) to the human being.[9] What does it mean then that in the *Ge-Stell*, that is, in the imposition of the technical world, there flashes this play of appropriation-transpropriation which makes up the event of being? The fact is that the *Ge-Stell* as the whole of ordering is not characterized only by planning and by the tendency to reduce everything to *Grund*, to foundation-bottom (*fondamento-fondo*), and therefore to the exclusion of any historical novelty. But precisely insofar as the whole of ordering, the *Ge-Stell* is also essentially *Heraus-forderung*, pro-vocation. For in the world of technology, nature is continually provoked, made to serve ever new tasks, and human beings themselves are always called upon anew to engage in yet newer activities. Therefore, if on the one hand technology (*la tecnica*) seems to exclude history (insofar as everything is potentially preplanned), on the other this immobility of the *Ge-Stell* displays a dizzy character in which there exists a continuous reciprocal provocation between human beings and things. This aspect can be designated with another Heideggerian term, that of *Reigen*, or round-dance (*ridda*). In the last page of the essay on "The Thing,"[10] Heidegger connects the *Reigen* to the *Gering* (with the triple meaning of lowest, ring, and fighting, *Ge-ring*) of the world as *Geviert*, as fourfold. The *Ge-Stell* places being-there in a situation in which "our whole human existence everywhere sees itself challenged (*provocato*)—now playfully and now urgently, now breathlessly and now ponderously—to devote itself to the planning and calculating of everything."[11] All this urging of the technological challenge in which our historical experience is—*wesentlich* (substantially)—thrown can also be called the *shaking* (*scotimento*) (there may be here some possible references to Simmel, as well as to Benjamin's artistic shock). Now, in the same pages from *Identität und Differenz* we are here recalling, the *Er-eignis* is defined as "that realm, vibrating within itself, through which human being and being reach each other in their nature, achieve their active nature by losing those qualities with which metaphysics has endowed them."[12] Determinations or qualities assumed by human beings and being in the course of metaphysics are, for example, those of subject and object. Or, as Heidegger remarks later on in this same text, those that have determined the twentieth-century distinction between natural sciences and humanities, physics and history,[13] the division, that is, between a realm of spiritual freedom and a realm of mechanical necessity. It is precisely these contrasting determinations that are lost in the round-dance of the *Ge-Stell*. Things lose their rigidity insofar as they are wholly absorbed within the possibility of total planning, and they are provoked or challenged to ever new uses (without any reference to an allegedly natural "use value"). Besides being a subject, within this general planning the human being also turns into an object, liable to universal manipulation. All this does not only configure a demoniacal relevance of technology. Actually, precisely in its ambiguity there is the flashing of the *Er-eignis*, of the event of Being, as the disclosing of a horizon of oscillation in which the self-giving "of something as something," the "appropriation" of beings (*enti*) each in their definiteness, takes place at the expense of a permanent trans-propriation. Universal manipulability (of things and of being-there) does away with the traits that metaphysics had attributed to being and the human being. Above all, it does away with the stability (immutability, eternity) of being as opposed to a problematic realm of freedom in a state of becoming. To think technology not only as such but in its *essence*, Heidegger says, means to experience the challenge of universal manipulability as the recalling of the appropriating (*eventuale*) character of being. In the first of the two essays that make up *Identität und Differenz*, dedicated to the principle of identity, there is a dense network of connections between the description of the *Ge-Stell* as the place of the urging of challenge (*provocazione*), the description of the *Er-eignis* as a horizon of oscillation, and a notion which (as the second text on the onto-theo-logical constitution of metaphysics demonstrates) is central to the last phase of Heidegger's thought, namely, the notion of *Sprung*, leap or spring (to which we may also connect the notion of *Schritt-zurück*, the backward step). The thought which, according to the expression in *Zur Sache des Denkens* ("let go of being as foundation") in the sense of the hermeneutic foundation, is that thought which abandons the metaphysical horizon of representation in which reality unfolds on the basis of mediations and dialectical concatenations and which, precisely insofar as it escapes the chain of foundation, springs away from being understood as *Grund*.[14] This leap should lead us, Heidegger continues, there where we already are, in the constellation of human beings and being as configured in the *Ge-Stell*. The leap does not find, on arrival, a base upon which to stop; it only finds the *Ge-Stell* as the locus in which the appropriating character (*l'eventualità*) of being flashes and lets itself be experienced by us as the horizon of oscillation. Being is not one of the poles of the oscillating, which if anything takes place between being-there and beings (*enti*); it is the horizon (*ambito*), or the oscillation itself. The *Ge-Stell* may represent the utmost danger for thinking insofar as it develops to its ultimate consequences the implications of the metaphysical congealing of the subject-object relation. Yet, within technology as total organization, the *Ge-Stell* is also the locus of the flashing of the *Er-eignis* because universal manipulation, the provocation and shaking (*scuotimento*) that characterize it, constitute the very possibility of experiencing being beyond all metaphysical categories, first and foremost that of stability.

How does it come that the experience of the *Ge-Stell*, as briefly sketched, can configure itself as an example of "hermeneutic foundation?" Here we meet up again with the two elements which, as I suggested above, constitute Nietzsche's "God is dead," because:

1. The *Ge-Stell* is not a concept, it is a constellation of belonging, an event which *be-stimmt* all our possible experiences of the world; it serves as a foundation because, as in "God is dead," we receive its announcement;

2. but the belonging to the *Ge-Stell* serves as a foundation only insofar as it gives access not to an "*absolutum et inconcussum*" *Grund* but rather to a horizon of oscillation in which any belonging, any giving of anything as some such a thing, is tied to a movement of trans-propriation.

The hermeneutic character of the foundation which thereby comes into being seems to be linked primarily to the first of these two aspects. That is, as we realize that the conditions of possibility of our experience of the world are a historical-finite condition, a historically situated pre-comprehension. But, isolated from the second aspect, this foundation would merely be a distortion of Kantian transcendentalism into historicism. The genuinely hermeneutic character of the foundation is guaranteed instead by the second aspect we have indicated, which represents the nth metamorphosis of the hermeneutic circle referred to in *Sein und Zeit*.

Access to the *Er-eignis* as the horizon of oscillation is made possible not by technology, but by listening to its *Wesen*, which should be understood not as essence, but as enforcement (*vigere*), as a mode of self-giving, of technology itself. In order to think not of technology, but rather its *Wesen*, we need to take that step back of which Heidegger writes in the second essay of *Identität und Differenz* (it corresponds to the "spring" of the first essay), which confronts us with the history of metaphysics in its totality. One of the difficulties encountered in explicating the meaning of technology (*la tecnica*) and of the *Ge-Stell* in Heidegger (completion of metaphysics but also flashing of the *Er-eignis*) depends on the fact that his text does explicate further in what sense thinking the essence of technology—and therefore experiencing the *Ge-Stell* as the flashing of the *Er-eignis*—implies also confronting the history of metaphysics in its totality yet not from the perspective of a dialectical representation of such a history. It is legitimate to attempt to fill this void by recalling another text in which, once again, Heidegger speaks of spring. The pages of *Der Satz vom Grund* where we find that the principle of reason invites us to spring away from the *Grund* into the *Abgrund*, the abyss, which is at the bottom of our mortal condition. We do actually spring or leap to the degree that "we entrust ourselves to the liberating engagement in the legacy of thinking and . . . do so in a way that recollectively thinks upon it."[15] The access to the horizon of oscillation acquires therefore a further and more explicitly hermeneutic character. To respond to the appeal of the *Ge-Stell* entails also a leap that casts us within a liberating relation to the *Überlieferung* (tradition), that play of transmission of messages, of words, which makes up the only element of a possible unity in the history of being (which resolves itself entirely in this transmission of messages). Nietzsche had polemically described the nineteenth-century human being as a tourist who wanders in the garden of history as if rummaging through a closet of theatrical costumes which we can don and discard at will. And Heidegger has often called attention to the ahistoricalness that is proper to the world of technology, which, in reducing everything to a *Grund*, ends up losing the *Boden*, that is, any soil capable of giving rise to true historical novelty. But much like any other element of the *Ge-Stell*, the ahistoricalness of the technological world probably has also a positive valence. The *Ge-Stell* introduces us to the *Er-eignis* as the horizon of oscillation also and above all insofar as it dis-charges (*de-stituisce*) history of its *auctoritas*. History becomes not a dialectical explanation-justification of the present, and not even its relativistic devaluation (which would still be tied to the metaphysical contraposition between value of the eternal and nonvalue of what is transient), but rather the locus of a circumscribed cogency (*cogenza limitata*), of a problematic universality like that of Kant's judgment of taste.

Heidegger's meditation on the *Ge-Stell* thus looms as a first indication toward an ontology of decline, though still in embryo. Summarizing, this takes place along these lines:

1. The *Ge-Stell* lets the *Er-eignis* flash as the place of oscillation, setting us out thus to recover being not in its metaphysical traits, but in its "weak" constitution, oscillating *in infinitum*.

2. To gain access to being in this weak sense is the only foundation thinking can attain. It is a hermeneutic foundation, both in the sense that it looks at the horizon within which beings (*enti*) come to being (what used to be the transcendental in Kant) as a thrown historical-finite project and in the sense that the oscillation unfolds precisely as the suspension of the cogency of the present in relation to tradition, in a re-ascending that stops at no alleged origin.

3. Re-ascending *in infinitum* and oscillation are accessible through a spring which is, at the same time, a leap into the *Abgrund* of the mortal constitution of being-there. Otherwise said, the liberating dialogue with the *Überlieferung* is the true act with which being-there decides for its own death, the "passage" to authenticity referred to in *Sein und Zeit*. We as mortals can enter into, and take leave from, the play of the transmission of messages that the generations cast to one another, and which gives us the only available image of being.

These three moments make up what, for the time being. we wish to summon up with the formulation "ontology of decline." They are essential moments of Heidegger's heritage as they entail the indication of a positive theory of Being characterized as weak with respect to the strong being of metaphysics, as an endless re-ascending with respect to the *Grund* and the indication of the hermeneutic foundation as the kind of thinking that corresponds to this non-metaphysical characterization of being; and, finally, the peculiar connection of this non-metaphysical mode of the *Wesen* of being with the constitutive mortality of being-there.

If we now consider that *Sein und Zeit* had started out, among other things, from the need of individuating a notion of being that would enable us to think not only of the objects of science in their idealized eternity, but also of human existence as historically laid out between birth and death, we become aware that it is precisely an ontology of decline which, in the last analysis, answers or corresponds to the plan outlined in 1927. In the end, it appears that Heidegger's thinking can be summarized in his substitution of the idea of being as eternity, stability, force, with that of being as life, maturation, birth, and death. What *is* is not what persists (*permane*), but rather what, in an eminent sense (in the way of Plato's *ontos on*), becomes—that is, is born and dies. The assumption of this peculiar nihilism is the true realization of the program indicated by the title *Being and Time*.

3

Heidegger and Poetry as the Decline of Language

A great many practitioners of what, in contemporary aesthetics and criticism, we call the imperialism of the signifier—which exploded with structuralism and is still present in some exponents of post-structuralism, like Derrida and Lacan—make undue recourse to Heidegger, in the sense that they rely on a reductive interpretation of his theory on the relationship being-language.

A closer reading of this aspect of Heidegger's thought which would bear in mind the role he assigns to silence, can help us sketch new pathways for thinking, especially since there are ample signs that the imperialism of the signifier has overstayed its time and is fast on its way to dissolution.

Poetry and Foundation
"*Was Bleibet aber, Stiften die Dichter*"

"That which lasts is founded by the poets" is a well known line from Hölderlin which Heidegger comments upon extensively in the essay "Hölderlin and the Essence of Poetry."[1] This text can be taken as representative of Heidegger's thesis on the founding, inaugural character that is proper to art and specifically to poetry as the art of the word. The text where the commentary on this verse by Hölderlin appears belongs to the production of the so-called "second (or later) Heidegger" (the text dating to 1936), and that means a phase of his philosophy during which he develops most intensively the relation between language and being. This relation will come out in a scandalous fashion in some famous pages in the "Letter on Humanism" (1946), where Heidegger defines language as "the house of being," in both the objective and subjective sense of the genitive. The relation though has roots in the development of the notion of world in *Sein und Zeit*. In that earlier work, against the dominant idea that the world is the sum of all objects encountered in experience, Heidegger submits the thesis whereby the world comes before "single things," as it is the horizon of references within which something can be thematized "as some thing," as a determined being (*ente determinato*). Analyzed in depth, the context-horizon appears not as a structure of relations among things, but as a system of meanings. That, as it exists, being-there already has a world does not mean that it is in a direct relation with all things. Rather, it means that it is familiar with a system of signs and meanings. We could say, being-there already has a language available to itself. In this perspective, being means, for things, their belonging to a totality of references that is given above all as a system of meanings.

Heidegger's subsequent development of the theme of language, culminating with the text on humanism and then in *Unterweg zur Sprache*, can be considered rigorously coherent with the premises worked out in *Sein und Zeit*: the happening or event of being gives itself in language. The only difference is that any humanistic pretense, if it were ever there, is discarded. If the human being is a thrown project (see *Sein und Zeit*), "what casts, in the project, is being" (see *Über den Humanismus*), and not the human being. In its typical structure of reciprocal dependence—human beings speak of language, but it is language that "avails itself" of human beings as it conditions and delimits the human possibilities of experience, The relation between being-there and language becomes the place ("*luogo*") where one can grasp the relation of human beings with being, which is also characterized by a reciprocal dependence. However, we are not dealing merely with an analogy between these two relations—human being/language, human being/being—as *being is nothing except its self-giving in language*, or, otherwise put, *being is nothing other than the self-giving of language*. There is only one event, for both being and language.

Yet not all language acts are entitled to being an event of being. We can say that the event of language is the event of being only as the happening of being is thought, in Heidegger's terms, as the disclosing of the openings within which beings (*enti*) come to being. We can speak of a happening (*accadere*) of being, or as a happening of truth, as the context of meanings within which things and their references *are* is something that *gives itself* (*es gibt*) historically. It is significant that, beginning with the essay on "The Origin of the Work of Art" (1936), published in *Holzewege*, Heidegger no longer speaks of *the* world (as he did in *Sein und Zeit*), but of *a* world, suggesting that we can speak of it in the plural as well.

Historical worlds are the concrete openings and the concrete (though time and again diverse) contexts of signification and languages in which things come to being (and not, instead, a transcendental smokescreen of the "I think," as claimed by a certain strain of Kantianism pervading twentieth-century philosophy). Of being, one cannot say that it is, but that it happens (*accade*). Its happening is the instituting of the historical openings, we could even say of the fundamental traits, of the criteria (for true and false, good and evil, etc.) on the basis of which the experience of a given historical humanity is at all possible. But if this is the case, if being is not what happens in this sense, then we should be able to indicate the inaugural events that break the continuity of the preceding world and found a new one. These inaugural events are language events, and their site is poetry.

This is not the place to discuss whether and to what degree this conception of poetry as the inaugural event of a historical world manifests a Romantic emphasis. In any case, one could object that such a Romantic emphasis does not belong exclusively to Heidegger, since contemporary poetics and aesthetics are generally in agreement in recognizing that poetic language manifests a more radical originalness (*originarietà*) than everyday language. This view belongs also to the most radically formalist and even structuralist wings. What bears reflection, is that in this theory of the ontologically founding relevance of poetic language, Heidegger supplies the premises for freeing poetry from its enslavement to the referent, from its subjection to that purely representational (*raffigurativo*) concept of the sign which dominated the mentality of the metaphysical-representationalist tradition. By assuming the relation language/reality as a representational relation, traditional aesthetics would then follow through with the necessity to qualify poetic language, specifically with reference to certain kinds of content (for example, emotions) or certain purely formal aspects (for example, the verse). Twentieth-century poetics have definitively shunned these perspectives. And though they rarely subscribed explicitly to Heidegger's ontological position, they did move in a direction that presupposes the refusal of the representational dependence on things. It is precisely with reference to these, and more pointedly avant-gardist, poetics that Heidegger is to be credited with having unfolded most fully the ontological basis of their revolutions, showing which conception of Being to adopt if one really wants to exit from the representational mentality of metaphysics.

The happening of being is the instituting of the essential traits of a historical world. This instituting is the instituting of a language. And a language opens and institutes itself in its essential novelty in poetry. "What lasts is founded by the poets." It is in poetic language that being originally happens. This means that one can never encounter the world except in language. A summation of this thesis can be seen in Gadamer's statement in *Truth and Method*—a text where Heidegger's heritage is most alive—in which "being that can be understood is language (*Sein, das verstanden werden kann, ist Sprache*)." The happening of being is, in the last analysis, *Überlieferung*, the transmission or tradition of linguistic messages. In this light, it would then seem impossible to carry out Husserl's program, from which Heidegger too started out, of going "to the things themselves." With the exception of Gadamer, contemporary thought has interpreted Heidegger's identification of being and language as affirming an insurmountable absence of being, which could only and always give itself as *trace*. This affirmation of the absence and the trace can be made either because of a residual nostalgia for the present, as we see in Derrida and Lacan, or from the point of view of freeing the simulacrum from any reference to and nostalgia for the original, as in Deleuze. In both cases, the thesis of the identity of being and language is read as the liquidation of any possibility to refer to an "originary" in favor of a conception of experience which moves only on surfaces, whether by longing for the original and considering itself decayed and alienated, or by enjoying the freedom thus granted in a sort of delirium of the simulacrum.

Although Heidegger can underwrite the thesis summarized in Gadamer's statement that "being that can be understood is language," nevertheless he does not renounce thinking about a possibility of access to the originary, and therefore about the possibility of carrying out somehow Husserl's program. This is precisely what Derrida criticized him for in some of the pages from the conference on "*La différence*."[2] This marks a crucial distinction between the French thought of *différence* and Heidegger's position, both at the level of philosophy in general and as concerns the thinking of poetry. For Heidegger, it is true that "what lasts is founded by the poets." Yet the foundation that poetry works out is not under the power of the poets.[3] It is true that, as we shall see, in Heidegger's way of understanding the foundation there subsists also a peculiar play of degrounding—this is not, however, in the sense of a definitive renunciation to any possible relation with the originary. Poets found what lasts, but they are in turn "founded." The foundation is such "not only in the sense of the free act of giving (on the side of the poets), but at the same time in the sense of the firm basing of human existence on its foundation."[4]

Authentic Word and Silence

"*Weil ein Wortklang des echten Wortes nur aus der Stille entspringen kann. . . .*" ("A resounding of the authentic word can only usher forth from silence.")[5] Poetry inaugurates a world, discloses and finds what lasts, only as it in turn responds to an appeal. Its ability to initiate is therefore relative. In this, Heidegger's thought does not tolerate being reduced either to the Derridian-Lacanian philosophy of absence or to Deleuze's philosophy of the simulacrum. Poetry's inaugural ability to initiate is neither a departure that leaves behind a *béance*, an emptiness that is never filled, nor is it a pure production of differences through the repetition of an original which is not there and whose absence is not even felt. Heidegger can speak of an "*echtes Wort*," an authentic word, precisely because according to him the form of access to the originary is not only negative. Whereas the philosophy of absence is interested in affirming the constitutive absence of being, in terms of a metaphysical description (that is, being *is* absence), and whereas the philosophy of the simulacrum is interested above all in liquidating, through the notion of a different repetition, any reference to an original-originary, Heidegger wants to remain loyal to *difference*. The access to the originary is for him the access to difference. It is the originary that, in its difference from those beings that are present in the world, constitutes the horizon of the world, *be-stimmt* it, determines it, tunes it, delimits and sizes it up in its constitutive dimensions. In order for the differences inherent in the world to unfold, in order that a world be given—articulated primarily through language—it is necessary that somehow the *other than the world* (*l'altro dal mondo*) be given: being as other than beings, the originary as other than mere spatio-temporal entities, or even still, *An-wesen-lassen* as other than simple *An-wesen*.[6] It is only this self-giving on the part of the other-than-beings that divests the mere entity of the world of its peremptoriness, of its imposition as the only possible set up for beings. In differentiating itself from beings, being serves as origin (*principio*) of an *epoché*, a suspension of the approbation to the world as it is, and therefore also as origin of all possible changes. In order to serve as origin of the happening of the new, as possibility for new epochal openings, being must somehow give itself, it must be accessible, though this does not mean it must give itself over in presence. The world in which thought can have access to being, conceived not as an entity itself but as that which makes beings (*enti*) be, is *Andenken*, remembrance or recollective thinking.

Andenken is that thought which recollects being as what is different, which "think(s) of the difference as such,"[7] that is to say, it thinks being as what does not identify itself with beings (and thus can always work as an instance of judgment upon them) and thus differs them. It makes beings differ by disclosing the differing dimensions of the world, and dislocates beings. Under the first aspect, *Andenken* can also be called critical or utopic thought. This associates Heidegger to those currents in contemporary philosophy that vindicate the critical relevance of thinking and describe the negativity of the present human condition in terms of the loss of the capacity to refer to alternative instances with respect to the present-day configuration of beings. This is what, in Heidegger's terms, is called *Seinsvergessenheit*, the oblivion of being.

But the critical capacity of thinking demands that it have a possibility of somehow gaining access to the originary. This possibility is the relation entertained with silence. "A resounding of the authentic word can only usher forth from silence." The authentic word is the inaugural word, the one that lets truths happen, that is, lets new openings of historical horizons occur. The relation of the authentic word to silence is not based on its need to have a background from which to emerge. To speak authentically, instead, means staying in a relation with the other than the signifier, with the other than language. This is the reason why elsewhere Heidegger writes that "authentic saying" cannot but be "a simply keeping silent about silence."⁸ It would not be difficult to render this harsh Heideggerian statement more "acceptable" by showing its likely relations to Saussure's distinction between *langue* and *parole*, for example, with all the variations it has known within contemporary aesthetics and poetics. The inaugural act that produces a modification *of the* code cannot come from a pure movement within the code itself. On another plane, even the popularity of the concept of revolution in our contemporary culture, even at the level of everyday talk, shows thinking's willingness to recognize that radical changes stemming from agents outside the system (such as the proletariat, supremely alienated and thus capable of being the universal class) are possible. In this light, the possibility of an originary word as theorized by Heidegger corresponds to the possibility that there is a true happening (*accadere*) within history, contrary to what is implied in the dogmatism of simple presence that has always dominated metaphysics (from which the profoundly "anamnestic" historicism represents the most up-to-date version, as Ernst Bloch has shown). This possibility demands that there be a relation with the *other*, to which Heidegger alludes with the term "silence."

Being-Towards-Death and Silence

"*Das Wesenverhältnis zwischen Tod und Sprache blitz auf, ist aber noch ungedacht*" ("The essential relation between death and language beckons, but is not yet thought").⁹ The relation of language with silence can be understood only if we recall the double function, founding-degrounding, which being-towards-death has for Heidegger since *Sein und Zeit*. In that work, as is well known, being-there is finally constituted as a whole, that is, it can confer a historical continuity to its own existence but only as it projects itself towards its own death. This is one of the most intricate points, even at the terminological level, of *Sein und Zeit*, where Heidegger explicitly picks up elements from the religious and metaphysical tradition. Death is defined by Heidegger as the permanent possibility of the impossibility of all other possibilities on this side of it which make up existence. These possibilities can be linked in a continuum, in a mobile context lived as history, but only if they do not become absolutized, if being-there in short does not assume any of them as unique and definitive. What allows us not to absolutize the single possibilities—thus producing an unsurmountable discontinuity in existence—is the anticipatory decision for one's own death. Placed in relation to death, the possibilities of existence reveal themselves and are lived as pure possibilities. Being-there can go on from one to the other in discourse, and existence becomes a tissue-text, a continuity of references, of retentions and protensions. The very passing of time, tied as it is, in *Sein und Zeit*, to the self-projecting of being-there and to its going back over its own past, is disclosed in the end only by this anticipation of death.

We can thus perceive the essential relation between language and death which Heidegger declares "is not yet thought." The world, in fact, discloses itself in its essential dimensions through language. On the other hand, the self-articulation of the dimensions of the world means above all the unfolding of the three temporal ecstasies of past, present, and future. Let us turn to an elementary example. The relation image-background (*figura-sfondo*), the model against which we can think the thematization of anything *as some thing*, that is to say, any appearing of beings within the horizon of the world, is not above all a spatial fact, but rather it is a temporal fact (in the sense in which Kant attributes a greater originary character to time as opposed to space). There is no disclosing of the world except as the instituting of a language. Yet, on the other hand, language does not unfold, ultimately, but in time (and as time), which temporalizes itself only beginning with the anticipatory decision for one's own death.

The decided anticipation of death as the possible impossibility of all possibilities on this side of it serves ultimately as the foundation of language, of temporality, of the horizon of the world, and of existence as historical continuity. But if this foundation occurs with reference to death, then this means also that being-there is constituted as a continuous whole only with reference to an essential *discontinuity*. Being-there can be a whole (*un tutto*)—that is, it can have an existence as a texture of events, words, and meanings—only as it decides in favor of its own nullification. History can happen as history only as it relates to nothingness. This is what Heidegger says in some conclusive pages from *Der Satz vom Grund*. The principle of sufficient reason, which calls us to assign a cause to each thing, that is, to constitute the world of experience as a context (of causes and effects, but also of references and significations of all sorts), is also the appeal of an *Abgrund*, of an abyss that shows us, at the base of the continuity of experience, death, and nothingness.

At the base of every foundation, even the one worked out by the poets "who found what lasts," there is an abyss of degroundedness (*sfondatezza*). The poet's founding language really founds only if and insofar as it is in relation with that other of itself that is silence. Silence is not merely the resonant horizon needed by the word *resound*, that is, to constitute itself in its consistence as being: it is also the bottomless abyss in which the word, once uttered, *loses itself* (*si perde*). Silence is to language what death is to existence.

Silence and the Sacred

"*Das Heilige ist durch die Stille des Dichters hindurch in die Milde des mittelbaren und vermittelnden Wortes gewandt*" ("The sacred, through the silence of the poet, is transformed by the mildness of the mediated and mediating word").[10] The bottomless abyss of silence, in which the word is lost, is however indicated positively by Heidegger by means of names. For example, in the comment on Hölderlin's poem "*Wie wenn am Feiertage . . .*" the names are *Physis*, Chaos, and the Sacred. In that text, the Sacred is not preferably related to the divine because the Sacred is also "above the gods" (EH 58), as it is the unitary horizon within which gods and mortals can appear. In this originary sense, which precedes the very distinction between mortals and divinities, the Sacred can be also referred to with the term *nature*, *physis*, or with that of Chaos. "Chaos is the Sacred itself" ("Chaos is the holy itself" in EH 85). The names Chaos and *physis*, which Heidegger uses to articulate the notion of the Sacred in his commentary on Hölderlin, serve to qualify such a notion in a substantial way, removing the impression of a generically religious undertone in his conception of poetry.

In the sense employed by Hölderlin and then by Heidegger in his commentary, *nature* counts as much as the originary Greek term *physis*, which Heidegger reads with reference to the notion of *Wachstum*, or growth. But this is neither in the sense of evolution nor in that of a pure sequence of events brought one near to the other. "*Physis* is an emerging and an arising, a self-opening, which, while rising, at the same time turns back into what has emerged, and so shrouds within itself that which on each occasion gives presence to what is present" (EH 79).[11] "*Physis* is the rising returning within itself" (EH 79). The sense of the growth model seems here to be above all the recalling of a temporality that cannot be understood as a chronological succession, or even as a process finalized toward some completion. *Physis* understood as growth is thought as lived (or living) time, which is after all the driving force already in *Sein und Zeit*. We recall that the temporal horizon in which beings are cast is essentially qualified by the mode in which the concrete human subject, being-there, does in fact live temporality, that is, in terms of *Sorge* (care) and *Befindlichkeit* (affectivity or emotive situation). Lived time coincides with the horizon and, in the last analysis, with being itself. Being is not in fact the substance of the image (*figura*), but rather the whole image/background (*figura/sfondo*) and the articulating of this whole. Such an articulating is temporal, but a temporalizing for which already *Sein und Zeit* employs the verb *zeitigen*, the common meaning, even before Heidegger's specific emphasis, is actually the coming to maturity, ripening. It is the horizon and the articulating of image and background, being is time, and more specifically growth, lived time, "maturing."

The notion of growth corresponds neither to the idea of time as pure succession nor to the notion of time as development toward a final condition. Even in this latter case one would have to presuppose a juxtaposition of moments considered as initially separate (the *telos* assigns a sense to the process only if it is thought of as preceding the process itself). To think *physis* as the Sacred that is given through the silence of the poet is to think *physis* on the model of living life. We cannot not connect this to Heidegger's insistence on being-towards-death. Through the poet's silence there speaks a Sacred that is nature as growth, as lived temporality. As it appears especially in *Sein und Zeit*, lived temporality is profoundly marked by being-towards-death. What is thus outlined is a connection between the Sacred, *physis*, living time, being, and being-towards-death. The problem of the language-silence relation should also be seen in their light.

But before returning to this relation, let us further recall that, together with that of *physis*, the other name Heidegger employs in this text to indicate the Sacred is Chaos: "For every experience which knows only what is mediated, Chaos seems to be the absence of distinctions, and therefore pure and simple confusion." However, "thought on the basis of *physis*, Chaos remains that aperture beginning with which the opening opens, so as to guarantee to each distinct its circumscribed presence" (EH 61). In this way, Chaos is divested of the negative and confusing traits which it has in the everyday sense. Nevertheless, for experience, Chaos remains also a danger and a risk in need of mediations. In the pages we are commenting on, Heidegger analyzes also the condition of the poet in terms of risk precisely because the poet's role is that of setting the world of articulated experience, of mediations, in relation to originary Chaos, that is, to the wide-opened opening of the Sacred. From the point of view of its relation with the Sacred as Chaos, poetry appears indeed to be a descending movement, which mediates and transforms the Chaos-Sacred into the *Milde*, into the gentleness of the communicable or communicated spoken word. But it is also always an ascending movement in which the poet, encountering being as *physis* and lived temporality, encounters his or her own being-towards-death, the radical alterity which is handed over to him or her as *nothingness* and *silence*.

The happening of the word entails a risk because the other than language is not only the silent background against which the word resounds, nor is it only the silence that scans the intervals and differences between words. Rather, in a positive sense, it is the silence of lived temporality that has death as its limit and constitutive foundation. *Physis* is therefore indeed nature, but in a sense which has nothing banally "naturalistic" about it. And yet—since in the term *physis* being is thought of as lived temporality, open onto death—the other than language, the silence of the poet, is also somehow the silence of *animal life*. In Heidegger's statement that "authentic saying" is "to keep silent about silence," there is also present something that harks to animality. After all, in the often cited comment to the poem "*Wie wenn am Feiertage* . . ." Heidegger cites from another of Hölderlin's text, "*Die Titanen*," the expression "*die heilige Wildniss*," the "sacred wood" (EH 61). This can indeed be taken as Chaos, as the opening that makes possible the circumscribed differences of experience. But it also qualifies, and in a positive light, as "wild" the other than language, alluding to a founding/degrounding of culture in the direction of "nature" entirely conceived as the growing that discloses itself in the lived temporality opened onto death.

Being and Westering of Language

"*Ein 'ist' ergibt sich, wo das Wort zerbricht*" ("Where words break off some thing may be").[12] The foundation, accomplished by poetry, of "what lasts," of the world as the articulating of dimensions of experience that open up especially through language, happens at the expense of a *degrounding* that the poet experiences, and which confers inaugural force to his or her poetry. Only as they expose themselves to the setback of the *Abgrund*, of the abyss of Chaos and silence, do poets disclose and ground the order of meanings that make up the world.

Contemporary poetry has often believed it had to rid itself of this romantic and then existentialist conception of poetizing. It did so by leaning on an idea of poetic language that, primarily through the formalistic categories of self-reflection and ambiguity, becomes the means by which the subject reappropriates language and exits the linguistic dispersion and alienation experienced in everyday banality. The inaugural meaning of poetry has thus been recoded to a more acceptable function as a sort of "gymnastics of language" which, by manifesting the linguistic mechanisms, the hidden possibilities, the limitations in a sort of abstract purity, prepares for its "better" and more conscientious use on the part of the speakers. It is like promoting gymnastics among the populace in order to attain a healthier race and greater labor productivity. Except that—just to stay within the gymnastics example—to call people's attention on the body could also have the perverse effect of unleashing uncontrollable processes of sensual intensification and in general of narcissism, with the consequent augmented refusal of both work and social discipline.

In a sense only very remotely parallel to this example, we see unfolding in Heidegger what could be called the "dialectic" of founding and degrounding (*fondamento e sfondamento*). Being is indeed *physis* constituting the temporal horizon upon which beings (*enti*) distinguish themselves, but it is also the Chaos of the sacred *Wildniss* manifesting the definitive foundationlessness of any foundation, opening the possibility of new foundations but also marking them all with the unsurmountable trait of nothingness. We cannot, from Heidegger's standpoint, set in motion the inaugural and foundational function of poetic language, and therefore also its self-reflexivity and role as a gymnastics of language (*lingua*) and reappropriation of language (*linguaggio*), without at the same time exposing ourselves to the encounter with nothingness and silence. On the basis of the connection between lived temporality and being-towards-death, we think that nothingness and silence can be legitimately understood not so much as some kind of divinity thought in terms of negative theology, as much as the *other*-than-culture, and therefore as nature, animality, the *Wildniss*, or even, if we prefer, the body and affectivity ahead and on this side of any alienating regulation managed by the symbolic in the Lacanian sense.

These are the contents of poetic silence. Silence certainly means that poetry must "return in the sound of silence which, as originary saying, sets in motion the regions of the *Geviert*" (EH 216), that is to say, the regions of the world originally "squared" in the relation among "earth and sky, mortals and divinities."[13] But it also means silence in the usual sense of the word. Poetry exercises the inaugural function that is proper to it alone not only as it "founds what lasts," but also as it "degrounds (*sfonda*)" this foundation in the lived relation with nothingness, with the other as *physis*, as animality, and as silence. In this way, the poetic word draws nearer to its own proper essence the closer it gets to silence.

From this vantage point, poetry can be defined as "decline of language" (*il tramonto del linguaggio*, a "westering of language"). And not as the establishment of a condition where there is no more language, but rather as the continued and ever renewed pushing of language to its extreme boundaries, where it shipwrecks in silence. This is what Nietzsche calls the musical and, in the last analysis, Dionysian essence of lyric poetry in opposition to epic as Apollonian poetry of sculpted definiteness. Once again, these theses seem to be marked by a romantic afflatus, whereas upon closer, unbiased inspection they instead reveal themselves to be an adequate description of the experience of twentieth-century poetry. The rarefaction of lyrical language, experimentalisms of various kinds, the search for a "zero degree" or, conversely, the proliferation of signifiers without any possible legitimation by the referent (that is, both the liquidation of metaphor and its delirium as pure simulacrum) cannot be adequately interpreted, in a way that is relevant for criticism and aesthetics as well as for militant poetics, solely as phenomena that create new codes. In other words, these are not pure and simple foundations of new languages that can be described in their formal characteristics, in their sociocultural connections, and in their probable psychological motivations. These phenomena, rather, are to be read always, and above all, as facts of the westering of language, to be linked to the set of phenomena (describable also in sociological and anthropological terms) that can be characterized as the decline of modern subjectivity (*tramonto della soggettività moderna*).

Beckett's "zero degree" as read by Adorno is not only that of a specific condition of poverty, of a "*dürftige Zeit*" (time of lack) in which we are condemned to live "after Auschwitz." The "reduction" of the language of poetry, in other words, is perhaps not only a question of impoverishment and loss, to be linked to all phenomena of violation of the human by a society ever more alienated and terroristic. This reduction probably delineates instead a utopia in which language and modern subjectivity decline (*tramontano*). It is difficult to say whether, according to Heidegger, the decline of language and the decline of the subject are a trait peculiar to our epoch alone, the epoch of the fulfillment of metaphysics. Certainly we cannot say that there exists an essence of human beings, of language, and of poetry that lasts always the same and above history and its vicissitudes. Therefore, when we say that poetry is in essence the westering of language, the engulfment of the word in the bottomlessness of silence (with all the implied references to lived temporality, death, animality), we are not describing the eternal essence of poetry, but neither are we describing only the way of being of poetry in our century. Here we are talking about the *Wesen*, the essence of poetry as it comes into being, or happens, today for us, and that is, in the only way in which poetry is, *west*. A declining or setting of language occurs in our entire experience of poetry: not only in the way in which we poetize today, but also in the way in which we experience poetry from the past. We can experience poetry only as the declining of language. This happens in multiple senses, which of course we need to determine in relation to the current critical methodologies. In order to indicate a preliminary path, poetry can be read as the decline of language, as suspension of the cogency of the Lacanian "symbolic" in a play of dis-identification that practically negates the alienating character of the imaginary, while it charges art and particularly poetry positively, with all those subversive traits Plato wanted to exorcise when kicking the poets out from his republic.

Not, therefore, as Stefan George's lines commented by Heidegger have it: "where words break off no thing may be" ("*non c'è cosa là dove la parola viene meno,*" literally, "there is no thing there where the word fails").[14] Or better yet, this too, since the word, and the poetic word in particular, has always a founding function with respect to any possibility of real experience; but more fundamentally, "An 'is' is given there where the word breaks off" ("*un 'è' si dà là dove la parola si infrange*"). The two utterances are not in opposition as if they were two alternative theses. They are rather the two poles of a founding/degrounding movement in which, in our experience, poetry has always engaged and which makes poetry, more fundamentally than the art (of the origin) of the word, the art of (the decline into) silence.

4

Outcomes of Hermeneutics

The position of hermeneutics within contemporary philosophy is uncertain, and in any case it has not yet been determined by a canonical historiography. There are valid reasons to line it up near analytic philosophy, at least in the stages where the latter emphasizes the analysis of everyday language and develops Wittgenstein's theory of "language games." Or we may place it near the rediscovery of those broadly understood "theological" components of existence (this is the hermeneutic path followed by Ricoeur). Finally, there is reason to see hermeneutics as a variation of the Frankfurt School critique of ideology. Without pretending to explore all of the its directions, what I intend to discuss here is a hermeneutic path which I believe is among the most interesting developments of the last few years (by and large the seventies). The intention is to show that this proposal in the end reduces some of the most original and revolutionary contents of hermeneutics to traditional (or in Heidegger's terms, metaphysical) philosophy, which it conversely had undertaken to critique and overcome.

～

One of the most characteristic theses, or perhaps definitely *the* most characteristic one, in contemporary hermeneutics is Gadamer's statement according to which "*Sein, das verstanden werden kann, ist Sprache*" ("Being, that can be understood, is language.")[1] There is no doubt in my mind that the statement is to be read with two commas, which at least in Italian exclude any restrictive meaning, as it would then be tautological. It is not (only) being (*essere*) that is the object of comprehension (for example, in opposition to causal explanation, etc.) that is language, but it is the whole of being that, as it can be understood, is identified with language. This indicates one of the characteristic traits not only of contemporary hermeneutics, but of modern hermeneutics in general, beginning with F. D. E. Schleiermacher—what in short we can call the "explosion" of hermeneutics. In fact, it is all of modern hermeneutics that in a more or less explicit manner makes a claim to universality. Gadamer's thesis, in this respect, does no more than to interpret and sum up this general tendency. It is first announced in Schleiermacher, in the new relation, where he points out between *subtilitas explicandi* (subtlety of explication) and *subtilitas intelligendi* (subtlety of understanding).[2] The ability to explain texts—and here we are talking primarily about the Holy Scriptures,—the *subtilitas explicandi* on which traditional hermeneutics has persisted, is always subordinate to the capacity to understand them, not only, obviously, on the part of the exegete who does the explaining, but in a more general sense. The discourse of the exegete or the preacher who explains the Scriptures is in fact directed to the *intelligentia* of his or her listeners. Every communication of meanings is therefore subject to an interpretative process, requiring interpretation. Already in Schleiermacher, hermeneutics is no longer, therefore, a discipline reserved for the explanation of texts particularly remote, or difficult, or decisive—as is the case with classical and juridical texts, and the Bible—but can be applied to any type of message, written or oral though it may be. The process of extending the "linguistic" character (better: the character "of language" ["*di linguaggio*"]) to all of experience, a process that culminates in our century's philosophy, finds its premises already in Schleiermacher's doctrine. It is probably only his attraction to the empiricist tradition, and more broadly the weight of the methodic model proper to the exact sciences, that can explain the fact that Dilthey, at the end of the nineteenth century, feels compelled to found two distinct camps, the "sciences of nature" and the "sciences of the spirit," thus raising a wall—wobbly and short lived—against the process of "explosion" of hermeneutics. At any rate, if, on the one hand, Dilthey's effort represents the attempt to delimit the respective fields—for which only a certain type of "being," the one turned toward "comprehension," could be identified with language—on the other, with his search for a critical foundation of the sciences of the spirit he sets the stage for that decisive step toward the generalization of hermeneutics, as it sets in motion the crisis of the very notion of foundation. Foundation means in fact having access to an ultimate point whose grasp can put us in possession of the entire field through the possession of the first principles on which such a field depends. But such a notion, already valid for Aristotle, for whom *episteme* reigns over a field whose principles and causes are known, has an irremediably technical meaning—it aims to ensure the practical control of reality—which no longer makes sense when we attempt to apply it to the sphere of human history, or of individual and social choices.

Through the difficulties ultimately encountered by Dilthey in his effort to rigorously "found" the sciences of the spirit, modern hermeneutics reveals its second characteristic beside what we have called the tendency to an explosion beyond its own limits (whether these are the limits of sacred exegesis, which are overcome starting with Schleiermacher; or those of the classical in general, of juridical texts, of historical documents, or perhaps, in the end, the very limits of speech-language). Next to this first tendency is that of putting in a quandary the very notion of foundation. This trait also is widely present since the origins of modern hermeneutics, that is, in Schleiermacher. In his work, the circularity typical of the interpretative process—the "hermeneutic circle" so crucial to Heidegger's *Sein und Zeit*—is resolved in an indefinite reciprocal referencing between grammatical interpretation (which is the one that brings the text back to language (*lingua*) and in general to its historical cultural connotations) and technical or psychological interpretation (which is the one that tries to understand a text with reference to an author's specific use of language, or to the means made available by the culture of the given epoch). The grammatical interpretation tries to explicate a text by situating it within the totality of the *langue* (one would say using Saussure's terminology) of a certain epoch—the psychological interpretation situates it within the totality of the author's personality. These two types of collocations ultimately refer circularly one to the other, and this circularity finds no conclusion, therefore, no foundation in the classical sense of the term, as Dilthey still used it. The inconclusiveness (and the nonconcludability) of this circle might be one of the deep, content-related reasons that explain the unfinished state of Schleiermacher's hermeneutics, which stopped at the level of an ensemble of essays, sketches, notes, constantly shuffled, picked up and modified without ever achieving a systematic format. The same classical argument of the hermeneutic debate of the late eighteenth century, which Schleiermacher expresses through the precept of "knowing the discourse as well as, and then better than, the author himself understood it," seems to hark to this same circularity (are the meaningful intentions of the author really an ultimate datum?[3] Up to what point are they not rather predisposed, forged, predetermined by the *langue*? The *langue*, however—and one should think of the other Schleiermacherian circle, between *Bedeutung* and *Sinn* (meaning and sense)—can be nothing except the crystallization of acts of speech accumulated over time, and thus of psychological variations worked out by individual authors, and so on. Such an argument therefore expresses, under a different guise, the constitutive vocation of hermeneutics to put in a quandary the notion of foundation. The hermeneutic tendency to deground (*sfondare*) is then egregiously exemplified in Gadamer's *Truth and Method* through his elaboration of the notion of truth and "experience of truth." The whole discourse of *Truth and Method* is in fact built around the recognition that under the influx of the methodic model of the positive sciences, modern philosophy has generally identified truth with method, be it the demonstrative method of mathematics, or, with the same valence, the experimental method of physics. What we must do now is to rediscover the experience of truth that one has outside these methodic contexts. In order to clarify the meaning of "experience of truth," Gadamer recovers and underscores the German term *Erfahrung* (experience) in the sense it has in Hegel and his concept of phenomenology as "science of the experience of consciousness." In general, says Gadamer, we can speak of experience of truth where there is true experience. In other words, there where the encounter with the thing produces an effective modification in the subject. Not in the sense of an empiricist seal that impresses itself on the mind as if it were a piece of wax, but in the sense of a transformation-integration of the new with everything old that already constituted consciousness. In this way, experience of truth is true experience, defining itself as an event that transforms, moves, and dislocates consciousness.

If this definition of *Erfahrung* is taken seriously and pushed to its ultimate consequences, we find that it reveals a radical degrounding element—the experience of truth in fact withdraws from all attempts to frame it as a constructive, cumulative, identifying process. Truth understood as "dislocation," or "becoming other" does not "found" in any of the senses that this term has had in the philosophic tradition. Conversely, if the model of dislocation is understood in the dialectic sense defined by Hegel, foundation and construction are saved, since dislocation is always thought as a return to itself. In this case, however, the hermeneutic notion of truth as "becoming other" loses much of its originality and theoretical force.

In the end, Gadamer remains loyal to the notion of truth as dislocation in the sense that the transformation undergone by the subject as it experiences truth is not brought back to the identity of a dialectical subject of a Hegelian kind; rather, it actually leads the subject "beside itself" ("*fuori di sé*"), involving it in a game that transcends the players and casts them in a more comprehensive horizon.[4] And this horizon transforms their initial positions in a radical manner. When the interpretative dialogue is an experience of truth and play in this sense, then there is no interlocutor in it who wins and reduces the other to him or herself. The hermeneutic fusion of horizons gives rise to a radically new *tertium*, which is play also insofar as it puts into play the interlocutors in their being.[5] Therefore, the hermeneutic vindication of an extra-methodic experience of truth ends up, once again, in a movement of degrounding.

It is difficult to say up to what point, in Gadamer's own theory, there are elements that attempt not so much to recognize as to exorcise this movement.[6] This is a question though, that concerns not only or primarily the interpretation of Gadamer's theory, but rather the general sense of hermeneutics and of the philosophy that it entails.

We can understand some recent outcomes of the reflection on interpretation precisely as yet another effort to exorcise its degrounding tendencies. This applies above all to those outcomes that have developed from out of the reflection on the relation between hermeneutics and critique of ideology and that, in recent years, have revealed their fundamentally neo-Kantian inspiration. I am referring to the works of Karl Otto Apel[7] and to those, connected to Apel, of the more recent Habermas.[8] In order to point out the most salient traits of twentieth-century philosophy, which would join the two great currents identified as analytic philosophy (in a very broad sense, this means all Anglo-Saxon philosophy inspired by pragmatism, neopositivism, and neoempiricism, and existentialism—that is, continental thought not only strictly from the existentialist strain but also from phenomenology, ontology, and hermeneutics—Apel coined the expression "semiotic transformation of Kantianism."[9] Now it appears to me that, even though the semiotic transformation modifies Kantianism profoundly, it does not modify it enough to avoid that, in the end, the operation that turns into a Kantian modification of semiotics and hermeneutics. In very broad terms, what Apel means by the semiotic transformation of Kantianism is the fact that the a priori making experience possible have revealed themselves, through various ways in twentieth-century philosophy, to be facts of language (*linguaggio*) and not fixed structures of the cognitive faculty (categories, etc.).

Now, more radically than any other thinker in the twentieth-century, Heidegger conceives of the existence of the human being as being-thrown, which is being thrown from and into language (*linguaggio*). In *Sein und Zeit*, being-there (*esserci*) is the same as being-in-the-world. This in turn translates into being always-already familiar with a realm of signification (*significatività*). Being-there is not in the world as it actually touches all intrawordly beings (*enti intramondani*), but, rather, it exists as it is in relation with a network of references (*rimandi*) that unfolds and is given in language. We could say that to exist coincides with possessing a linguistic "competence," whatever that may be in any given instance.

On this Heideggerian premise Gadamer develops the thesis according to which "being, which can be understood, is language." Though partly for different reasons, both Apel and Habermas have reservations and objections concerning Gadamer's hermeneutics. Ultimately, these reservations and objections are inspired by the need that the "linguisticalness" ("*linguisticità*") of the horizons within which alone something is given "insofar as some thing" be more explicitly acknowledged as possessing all the traits proper to the Kantian transcendental and, above all, its normative measure. Much more than in Heidegger, in Gadamer the statement concerning the linguisticalness of experience seems sometimes to translate into a pure and simple transcription, on the level of language, of the historicity of being-there understood as mere intratemporality, in the manner of Dilthey's historicism. From Gadamer's perspective, history is the history of the transmission of linguistic messages, of the constituting and reconstituting of communicative horizons that are always, time and again, facts of language (*fatti del linguaggio*). But to hold this position, Habermas observed in his *Logic of the Social Sciences*, and above all to hold simultaneously, as does Gadamer, that the linguistic-hermeneutic character of experience is unrecognized (*misconosciuto*) by modern scientism (which was the same polemical target of Husserl in the *Krisis*), requires that we raise the problem of the reasons why. History does not appear as pure transmission of messages but rather lets emerge precisely those forms of opacity that are expressed in scientism, in ideology, in modes that, in short, seem to deny its primarily hermeneutic structure. If we just acknowledge the fact that intrahistorical communication, the construction and reconstruction of the horizons of dialogue among individuals, epochs, and societies, is hardly something untroubled, being rather a difficult and threatened enterprise subject to continuous risks of *Missverstehen* (misunderstanding that, already for Schleiermacher, is the normal starting point for all interpretative operation), it then appears clear that there is need to highlight the normative relevance of the linguistic-hermeneutic structure of experience. More than by Habermas, this task is carried out on the philosophical level by Apel.

According to Apel, if we recognize the linguistic-hermeneutic structure of experience, we must proceed by thematizing the *a priori of the unlimited community of communication* also as a normative function. That is, not only the horizons within which the ontic regions are given in their definiteness are linguistic horizons—they are, above all, communicative horizons in the sense that, according to a Wittgensteinean thesis that is central for Apel, a language game that cannot be played by a person alone. Whoever uses a language, even the most arbitrary one, plays according to rules, and such a person is always answerable for the observance of the rules to an (at least ideal) interlocutor (who may be the speaker him or herself, insofar as founder of the [language] rules which he or she must then obey.) Every language game is therefore a communicative game and therefore the semiotic transformation of Kantianism is also inevitably a hermeneutic transformation. We cannot thematize "something insofar as some thing," not even in the most elementary experience, without implicitly accepting the rules of a language and, above all, the rule that imposes respect for the rules. Yet to be answerable for the respect for these rules to an ideal interlocutor, or to a community of interlocutors, entails to immediately grant to these interlocutors the same rights and duties of the speaker. In this sense, the communicative community is unlimited and ideal, that is to say, necessarily thought as the possible locus for an exchange in which subjects are free from every opacity and obstacle imposed on communication by historical, social, economic, and psychological circumstances. The unlimited communicative community acts as an a priori on the theoretical plane—only by accepting the rules of the language games, and answering for their application, can I experience something insofar as some thing—as well as on the normative-practical plane. We can say that to found itself as possibility (in order to make sense), knowing (*la conoscenza*) requires that the communicative community, as the ideal tribunal before which effective language games are legitimated, serve also as an ideal in the sense of a *telos* that guides historical action (so that, once again, it may make sense). In sum: language games (in Wittgenstein's sense) have as their condition of possibility the "transcendental language game of the unlimited community of communication," which is, in the last analysis, the hermeneutic structure of experience. We possess a *Sprache*, a language and therefore a world only because, as the Hölderlin cited by Heidegger says, we are a *Gespräch*, a conversation. The hermeneutic dialogue, however, is given in the concrete historical dialogues as ideal norm and possibility to be realized, more than as an actual fact. In this way, Apel believes he has resolved the insufficiencies of Gadamer's theorization, which according to Apel does not account for the elementary fact that hermeneutics as explicit and reflexive "art" of interpretation always already presupposes a situation of "rupture" of communication. Above all, and related to the whole view, Gadamer put out of reach all those normative traits that have always characterized traditional hermeneutics, from the technical aspects of the various specialized hermeneutics (theological, juridical, literary), to problems relative to validity and the very broad relation to ethics.[10]

Today, the philosophical theme of interpretation seems to be addressed in the abovementioned form of a "theory of the unlimited communicative community" (Apel, Habermas) in addition to other forms such as the return to a technical sense of hermeneutics (for example, in the literary theory of H. R. Jauss)[11] and the vindication of the "theological" implications of hermeneutics (Ricoeur). In all three cases—Apel's indication of a "semiotic transformation of Kantianism," Jauss, and Ricoeur—what we have before us albeit in different senses and with different goals is a strong emphasis on the *constructive* or even *foundational* aspect of hermeneutics. Using Apel's position as a frame of reference, I would like to show that such an emphasis on the constructive aspect of hermeneutics forgets its degrounding element. What is thus lost is the reference to *finitude*, which (at least since Heidegger) is a characteristic trait of that philosophy focused on the phenomenon of interpretation.

This becomes immediately evident if we look closely at the motives inspiring the critique of Gadamer by Habermas and Apel. In his first and fundamental discussion of Gadamer in *Logic and the Social Sciences*, Habermas demands that theory account for the condition of "interruption of communication," and more specifically of social continuity, in which hermeneutics originates and operates. Elaborating this same position differently, Apel seeks a hermeneutic still rigorously linked to the problem of *validity*, from that specific to exegesis in the various fields all the way to ethics. In both cases, the solution seems to be that of bringing the hermeneutic structure of experience back to a Kantian transcendental "condition of possibility" that founds it in the sense that it makes it possible and, at the same time, legitimates it by furnishing it with norms, measures, and criteria for judgment and action. Habermas's demand is also here satisfied. Once we identify unlimited communication as the norm, we also open the way for recognizing the historical causes of the opacity that opposes its full unfolding; these causes can be legitimately described on the basis of the materialistic analysis of society. In such a way, however, it becomes clear that Habermas's and Apel's proposals are based on two concepts hardly reconcilable with the presuppositions of hermeneutics, especially in their Heideggerian elaboration. These two concepts can be indicated respectively as the idea of originary continuity and the idea of the self-transparent subject. These two concepts sum up the fundamental dogmas of modern rationalism, both in its Cartesian version (self-transparence) and in its Hegelian version (continuity). To ask *why* we need an art of interpretation and then demand an explanation regarding the origins of the condition of misunderstanding within which human existence unfolds means presupposing that the continuity—or the condition of undisturbed communication, of uninterrupted and nonproblematic social integration—be the normal state of existence. The subject that lives in this normal state of continuity and transparence is none other than the subject of C. S. Peirce's "logical socialism," to which Apel in fact explicitly refers. In other words, despite all efforts to deny the identification, such a subject is the ideal subjectivity of the scientist, who operates freely beyond the opacities and the historical-psychological conditionings impeding communication, who replicates scientific experiments in the purity and abstractness of the laboratories, and who then proves or disproves the validity of a general law. In truth, Apel makes this move and adopts the scientific subject as ideal not without justification. For him, the justification lies in the fact that in the modern world, and with the huge development of the social sciences, society has increasingly become the subject-object of science. The subject of the unlimited communicative community is therefore not the ideal construction of a Cartesian self but, rather, the subject that is concretely given (at least as a real possibility) in late-capitalist society. The semiotic transformation of Kantianism is not to be understood as an exclusively or mainly theoretical event, discovered by some thinker or school, because historically the importance of facts pertaining to communication and language has grown, at least in advanced industrialized societies. Social sciences develop within this context; with them, there also develops the actual possibility, for the social subject, of achieving self-transparency. This is the moment in which

> the communicative community which constitutes the transcendental subject of science becomes at the same time the object of science. . . . It becomes clear that, on the one hand, the subject of the possible consensus on scientific truth is not an extra-wordly 'general consciousness,' but rather real-historical society, on the other the real-historical society can be adequately understood only if it is considered a virtual subject of science, including social science, and only if its historical reality is constantly reconstituted in a manner both empirical and critical-normative, with reference to the ideal, to be realized, of the unlimited communicative community.[12]

The problem is: Is it true, as Apel claims, that all this "becomes clear?" We can ask the question differently: What happens, in this ideal of self-transparence, to the *passions* and *differences* of the subjects that enter the communicative process? We say passions and differences, but we could as easily say interests, options, or, in a word, *finitude*. The ideal of continuity and self-transparence of the subject completely repudiates one of the defining aspects of philosophical hermeneutics, at least in its Heideggerian version (which is the most appropriate and relevant), namely, the finitude of the subject. In order to avoid the risk of levelling everything onto paleo-existentialist themes, and also in order to underscore the unfeasibility of a religious solution, we should speak of degrounding (*sfondamento*) rather than finitude. But the meaning is the same, at least in the sense that the finitude of being-there is theorized in *Sein und Zeit* not as the basis for some unlikely reference to the absolute or the infinite, but as the recognition that existence is constitutively, essentially *ab-gründlich*, we could say, unfounded-abyssal. In the case of Apel and Habermas—but also, though we cannot take them up here, in Ricoeur and Jauss—we are confronted with a misunderstanding (*equivoco*) that is perhaps tied to the very essence of hermeneutics. Interpretation does in fact entail the risk (or at any rate the possibility) of being taken as an activity of deciphering, of retracing grounds and meanings that are hidden yet ultimately attainable. This seems to be precisely the case with Apel's and Habermas's conjoining of hermeneutics and the critique of ideology (with all the Hegelian echoes the latter brings to bear). After all, even in the structure (*impostazione*) of *Sein und Zeit*, hermeneutics seems initially to have this reconstructive and foundational meaning. The need to re-propose the problem of being beyond any possible confusion with the simple-presence characterizing beings (*enti*) means, and not even that implicitly, to heed the call to avoid reducing philosophy to the articulation of the actually given horizon or horizons (the "regions" of Husserl's phenomenology) by problematizing the very possibility of the horizons. In principle, this approach is not much different from that of the critique of ideology—the difference between being and beings can be identified with the difference between each specific utterance or the single contents of experience and the ideological presuppositions that are implicit and function as a base. What the critique of ideology and Heidegger's approach share (already in *Sein und Zeit* but especially later) is the thesis according to which the general traits that constitute the horizon within which beings become visible and the single experiences are made possible, are not eternal, but are qualified historically—*je und je*, each time again. Not only is being-there *there*, and has a world insofar as thrown; but its thrownness is also not dependent upon a structure of reason, being rather the radical historical qualification of all its projects of comprehension and interpretation of the world.

We come here to the closest proximity between Heidegger's thought and the intentions of the critique of ideology. Yet, we also encounter the point of their greatest distance. The problem of the difference between being and beings cannot be made entirely to coincide with the program of the critique of ideology because there is nothing, Heidegger claims, that can be called ideology insofar as there is no reference to what ideology is not (is it theory? is it science?) It is true that already *Sein und Zeit* speaks of the necessity to "destroy the history of ontology" (that is, of the thought that flattens being onto presence) and that the later Heidegger will attribute to metaphysics traits that resemble ideology and the Marxist notion of reification. But in reality, precisely in the wake of the rigor with which Heidegger stood by his fundamental thesis of the finitude (or: degrounding, groundlessness [*sfondamento, infondatezza*]) of being-there, it is impossible to find in him any reference to a continuity or a self-transparency of a subject that, as the positive pole opposed to ideology and reification, could justify the use of these terms.

Confronting the problem of the critique of ideology and more broadly the constructive elaborations of Apel and Habermas (which we have read as symptoms of a general tendency in contemporary hermeneutics) forces us to assess the full meaning of the degrounding of existence at the hands of Heidegger, especially in relation to the definition of hermeneutics as a specific philosophical position in the panorama of twentieth-century thought. What characterizes hermeneutics philosophically is precisely the nexus grounding-degrounding (*fondazione-sfondamento*), set in relief since *Sein und Zeit*. If this nexus is misunderstood or forgotten, the theory of interpretation loses its specific originality, falling back into philosophical horizons of a different nature.

The existential analytic of *Sein und Zeit* is, as a whole, a work of "foundation" of being-there as a hermeneutic totality. Only in this perspective can we understand and theoretically justify the question concerning the "possibility of being a whole" on the part of being-there that concludes the first part of the work and guides the layout for the second part. It makes no sense, in fact, to think that Heidegger asks the question simply out of need for a descriptive "completeness" of the phenomenon of existence. Although one may adduce reasons for understanding things in this way, the internal and even systematic content-related reasons for asking the question of the totality of being-there have to do with the fact that in the first section of the work, existence is described in hermeneutic terms. Husserl's motto, "to the things themselves," is taken there in the sense that things are really attained only if we have access somehow to the horizons in which something is given *as some thing*. These horizons are, more or less, the "regional ontologies" and, before that, fundamental ontology. It is this last one which responds to the question on the sense of being. Now, in *Sein und Zeit*, by means of the analysis of being-in-the-world, the sense of being reveals itself in its connection to the project that constitutes existence. Beings (*enti*) are given to being-there (*esserci*), that is, they come to being (*essere*), only within the horizon of a project. This projectual horizon is constituted for being-there only as it is projected as a *totality* (no beings can possibly give themselves except as instances within a system of references that coincides with the world). Ontologically, the world is "before" the individual beings that are part of it. From the point of view of being-there, being-in-the-world is being-always-already referenced to a totality of references or assignments.[13] This is what we can call the hermeneutic constitution of being-there. The totality of references is given to being-there only as familiarity with a system of meanings and certainly not with the unfolded actuality of the connections of tool-things: this is the sense of the important paragraph 17 of *Sein und Zeit*, on "Reference and Signs."

To speak of a foundation of this particular hermeneutic constitution of existence means asking how it is possible that there is such a *totality*, which is both the totality of the world as a concatenation of references and the totality of being-there itself. The response to such a question comes from the elaboration of the notion of being-towards-death. Being-there constitutes itself in its totality, in its authentic modality as well as in its inauthentic everydayness, only when it decides ahead of itself toward its own death. In the inauthentic existence of the *man* (the impersonal, everyday "they"), totality shows traits that we can call vague, "soft," of weak historicity, oscillating between the repetitive and the discontinuous (perhaps somewhat resembling a Kierkegaardian aesthetic stage?) because death is thought of as an event of the "they" (as idle talk has it, "they (people) die," "one dies"). In authentic existence, insofar as death is resolutely anticipated not as one possibility among others, but as one's own most possibility, being-there as project can constitute itself as authentic historicity. The anticipatory resoluteness toward death constitutes the possibilities of existence in their nature as *possibilities*, opening being-there to a *discursus* from one possibility to the other unmarked by any fracture or discontinuity. Existence is a fabric-text because the possibilities on this side of death open up as possibilities precisely through the resolutely accepted impending of their becoming impossible.

In such a way, the anticipatory decision for one's own death does indeed constitute existence as continuity of a discourse, of a text; the price of this, however, is its suspension over the non-ground (*non-fondo*), which is precisely the possibility of the impossibility of anything at all, in short, death. Being-there constitutes itself as a hermeneutic totality only by resolutely anticipating the possibility of not-being-there-any longer. The "vertiginous" sense of the hermeneutic circle—which we first saw at the origin of modern hermeneutics, in Schleiermacher—finds here its ultimate explanation, in the connection between hermeneutic totality and being-towards-death. Thinking that truly wants to correspond to this *ab-gründlich*, unfounded-abysmal, constitution of finite existence cannot limit itself to foundation as the constitution of totality. Thinking is truly "founded (*si fonda*)," and answers the question on the "sense of being," only if it opens itself to the call of the *Abgrund*, of the absence of foundation. The question on the sense of being, then, can be answered only by following the transformation of *sense* into *direction*—searching for the sense of being, being-there finds itself called in a direction that first dispossesses it, then de-grounds (*sfonda*) it, and finally makes it "spring" or "leap" into an abyss which is that of its constitutive mortality.[14]

The meaning of this recalling is exemplified by Heidegger's work on the history of the words of metaphysics in the years following the end of the 1930s. It is not a position of silence, but rather a retracing ad infinitum whose core is the etymological reconstruction of the *Leitworte* of Western metaphysics.

Is it reasonable to pit the apparent idleness, inconclusiveness, irresponsibility of this work on words, against the efforts of those who, like Apel, attempt to locate at the ground of the hermeneutic constitution of experience an a priori apparatus of a Kantian kind? Yes, it is, if it is true that the discovery of the hermeneutic constitution of existence implies the sidelining of any thought of foundation (and of the very notion of foundation). More than that, given that Apel's and Habermas's effort ends up bringing hermeneutics precisely in the horizon of this thinking.

Let us conclude, then, with some salient points that can be used to determine possible proximities, analogies, coincidences, and, above all, elements of irreducible contrast between the neo-Kantian "refoundational" project and the "main road" of contemporary hermeneutics as defined in Heidegger's and Gadamer's work:

1. What characterizes hermeneutics in Heidegger is the finitude of the thrown project that being-there is. Within the history of modern hermeneutics, this finitude announces itself through the ever returning thematic of the hermeneutic circle, which assumes in Heidegger its most radical form, that of the nexus between grounding and de-grounding in being-towards-death. It is being-towards-death that founds the hermeneutic structure of existence. This means also that the transcendental function of language that unfolds in the semiotic transformation of philosophy makes sense only within the perspective that ties it to the finitude of the project and to being-towards-death. In Apel's case, however, while correctly emphasizing the "transcendental" function of language, the semiotic transformation of philosophy brings this function within the perimeter of the metaphysical thought of foundation. It is therefore *only* a transformation, a reappearing of metaphysics that forgets the constitutive finitude of existence.

2. In Heidegger, the finitude of the project means its radical *historicity*. The horizon that gives meaning to entities, and in which things come to being, is never a stable structural a priori, but always a horizon historically constituted through the transmission and mediation of concrete linguistic messages. *Das Selbe*, that "same" of which Heidegger speaks in many of his later writings (such as *Vorträge und Aufsätze, Identität und Differenz*, and *Unterwegs zur Sprache*) *is not* a permanent metaphysical structure. It is, at most, a continuity that brings to mind the "family resemblances" theorized by Wittgenstein. In Apel's and Habermas's perspectives, historicity has only a negative function, that of constituting an opacity that is revealed as such in light of the a priori structure of unlimited communication, that is, a communication

that is ideally total, with no ambiguities or ulterior meanings or purposes. From this viewpoint, the content of the messages transmitted through the vicissitudes of generations is wholly irrelevant. What counts is their form, which exhibits the typical metaphysical relation of universal and particular. The theory of the a priori of communication is ideally aimed at the "experimental" subject of modern science, basically cleansed of any attachment to history, feelings, interests, and differences.

If these two juxtapositions (among many other possible ones) are valid, the theory of the a priori of communication does not seem to be a legitimate development of hermeneutics in the sense that it does not develop its characterizing element, namely, the philosophy of finitude. To the idea of foundation understood in a Kantian and therefore still metaphysical sense, Heidegger opposes a research that moves on the thread of the connection between grounding and de-grounding (*fondazione e sfondamento*). The thought of foundation is replaced with thinking as *An-denken*, as a back-tracking ad infinitum, as a leap into the *Ab-grund* of the mortal condition, which follows the network of historical-linguistic messages (from the past as well as from "other" cultures) that, in their calling out to us (crystallizing in the languages we speak and that order us), determine and define the sense of being as is given in our historical-destinal constellation (on the basis of Heidegger's nexus between *Geschichte* and *Geschick*, history and destiny). As back-tracking ad infinitum, *An-denken* becomes "re-appropriation," though not in the sense of the mastering (*presa di possesso*) (of the principles) of the real that characterizes grounding, but, rather, in the sense of a suspension, through de-grounding, of the alleged cogency of particular historical horizons that presume to exhaust the sense of being. Limitlessness too is to be found in *An-Denken*, but precisely as nonconclusiveness of the path (*percorso*). This back-tracking or retracing (*risalimento*), moreover, has to do with communication much more authentically than Apel's a priori: it does not in fact consider solely the structure of messages, or the form of their communicability, but pays close attention to their contents, which are time and again different and, in their concatenation, determining for our historical being. One might say that what counts are the specific etymological strings, and not the laws of phonetics or of transformational grammar.

It is precisely because it is so profoundly tied to the contents of historical transmission, of *Überlieferung*—contents which in their announcing and corresponding define the sense that being has for us—that recollective thinking is in the end bound to finitude as mortality. It is only because we are also *ontically*, that is, biologically and actually, mortal, that we are also, as Hölderlin says, "a conversation." This complex interplay of commemorating thinking *versus* foundation, being-towards-death *versus* permanent transcendental structures, "degrounding" (*sfondante*) suspension of the cogency of historical horizons *versus* the (inevitably dogmatic) critique of ideology, this complex game is perhaps the most original sense of the hermeneutic reflection, representing the core of its contribution (on which more work needs to be done) to twentieth-century thought.

Appendix 1

The Crisis of Subjectivity from Nietzsche to Heidegger

Nietzsche, Heidegger, and Postmodernity

The title of this chapter should not be understood in a narrowly chronological way, as if we merely wanted to explore the history of the notion of subjectivity during that period of philosophy that begins with Nietzsche and ends with Heidegger.[1] I believe that these two names mark out a unifying theoretical strand which indicates a continuous development transcending their different approaches or results. This development can have philosophical significance to the degree that it involves the destiny, the vicissitudes not only of the *notion* of subject in the two thinkers, but also of the subject itself in an epoch of which Nietzsche and Heidegger are here considered the supreme interpreters. In other words, our initial thesis is that there exists between Nietzsche and Heidegger a substantial theoretical continuity, and that they are basically saying the same thing. To acknowledge this "same thing" means pointing to certain conceptual parallels and analogies between the two thinkers and then proceeding to place these similarities within an epochal horizon in order to see them as modes of revelation of a destiny which concerns (our) subjectivity in the present age.

Obviously, we are not dealing with a set of neutral or descriptive premises. And if this is true for every discourse in philosophy—even the most explicitly programmatic study of sources and data—then it ought to be especially valid for thinkers like Nietzsche and Heidegger who described themselves as epochal thinkers: representatives of a way of thinking whose truth is also and perhaps above all the truth of an epoch. In this they resemble Hegel, though their tone is fundamentally critical-destructive rather than triumphant.

༄

The thesis concerning a concrete theoretical continuity between Nietzsche and Heidegger is not at all so evident if we recall how Heidegger himself considers Nietzsche the culmination of metaphysics and its inherent nihilism. Heidegger in fact considers it his task to go beyond metaphysics and nihilism, suggesting his radical discontinuity with the tradition that peaks in Nietzsche. Of course, in Heidegger's own texts dealing with this problem—in a sense, this means all his mature writing—the relationship between postmetaphysical thought and the nihilism of achieved (*compiuta*) metaphysics is not so clear-cut and schematic, and raises several interpretive problems. And while it is acceptable to call Nietzsche a nihilist, calling Heidegger one can seem scandalous. This issue could be developed at length.[2] Yet I feel that one of the most pressing tasks for philosophy today, one of its crucial theoretical aims, consists precisely in clarifying the ambiguities of the Nietzsche–Heidegger relationship, recognizing their profound continuity, the fact that they say the "same thing": nihilism.

If, as we hinted above, this continuity is not only a fact that can be inferred from the texts of these two philosophers, but also perhaps above all the result of a reflection on their epochal meaning, then clearly in this second sense we must, as good hermeneutists, fall back on a shared preunderstanding of the salient traits of our present epoch. This preunderstanding is, after all, what gave life to philosophy when it appealed to experience, which was never that imprinting of signs and traces on the mental *tabula rasa* of a distorted, schematic empiricism. Rather, preunderstanding is a historically qualified experience, knowledge of the world, familiarity and expectation, memory, language. So the thesis of the continuity between Nietzsche and Heidegger is based not only on their texts, but also on our preunderstanding of the meaning of our historical existence in the present age. Reflecting upon this continuity means, therefore, activating and deepening this preunderstanding which, though seemingly vague and indeterminate, is nonetheless the guide and support of all thinking processes. As the horizon of our experience, such a supporting (*reggente*) preunderstanding must remain by and large implicit, though it is important to remain aware of it and its possibilities. In fact, it can even be perceived through the several signs and symptoms of our discourse. For instance, the theoretical as well as experiential-epochal horizon within which we can speak of a Nietzsche-Heidegger continuity, together with the corollary of a Heideggerian nihilism, coincide with what hermeneutics calls the philosophical *koiné* of our epoch.[3] In other words, though we cannot once and for all give form to the contemporary *pre*-understanding which acts as the background of the Nietzsche-Heidegger continuity, we can certainly describe some of its traits more precisely.

One trait of contemporary preunderstanding is the demonstrable, pervasive presence since at least the mid-1970s of hermeneutics. This philosophy, which revolves around the problem of interpretation, harks back to Schleiermacher, Dilthey, Nietzsche, and Heidegger, and was developed in different directions but with shared concerns by philosophers like Gadamer, Pareyson, Ricoeur, Jauss, and Rorty, who contributes an explicit attention to pragmatism. Thus broadly understood, hermeneutics can include philosophers such as Karl Otto Apel, and most recently Habermas, Foucault, and Derrida, whose philosophies do not properly speaking belong to its main trunk yet are profoundly related to it. Above all, the hermeneutic *koiné* constitutes today not only a field for theoretical speculation, but the underlying methodological self-consciousness of much literary and art criticism and of many trends in history, psychology, and the social sciences. In short, the role and position of hermeneutics in contemporary European thought can be compared—though with different modalities and implications—to the importance of Marxism in the 1950s, and structuralism in the 1960s and 1970s.[4]

If this is the situation, then we are living in an age whose characteristic cultural atmosphere or mood facilitates the understanding of the Nietzsche–Heidegger continuity. In fact, above and beyond Heidegger's reading of Nietzsche, hermeneutics is the unifying thread of the two philosophies. I believe that in speaking of this relationship I am not necessarily endorsing some misguided historiography, or—as Habermas said of Gadamer—excessive "urbanization" of both Nietzsche and Heidegger, but the fact that there is indeed such a deeply rooted process in motion within our culture.[5] If it is to remain true to the imperative of "saving the phenomena" which has guided it since ancient times, then philosophical reflection must reckon with this fact of our everyday experience and must save it.

To conclude these prefatory remarks, it is likely that recognizing this concrete continuity between Nietzsche and Heidegger constitutes also the decisive trait of what we call the postmodern in philosophy. As will become evident shortly, this continuity actually points toward the dissolution not only of modern subjectivity, but also, and more generically, of being itself—no longer structure but event, no longer origin or foundation but calling and "narration" ("*racconto*"). This seems to be the sense of that devaluation (*alleggerimento*) of reality which is taking place in our lives, which are determined by those typically postmodern transformations of technology.[6]

From the Unmasking of the Subject to Nihilism

Within this perspective, let me dwell further on my title's crisis of subjectivity. If there is a difference between Nietzsche and Heidegger, it is this: Heidegger achieves that passage into postmodernity which Nietzsche merely announces and sets in motion. Yet there are parallels in their writings about postmodernity's crisis of the subject.

In Nietzsche the crisis of subjectivity is announced primarily as the unmasking of the superficiality of consciousness.[7] This is one of the meanings of *The Birth of Tragedy*'s distinction between Apollonian and Dionysian. Socrates, the champion of the Apollonian as what is definite, rational, disengaged from the Dionysian that myth, irrationality, sensuality, the experience of living and dying is also the champion of self-consciousness. How else to justify his "knowing that he does not know"? But it is precisely to the degree that he absolutizes, distancing himself from his mythical, irrational, vital Dionysian roots to assume the task of a global *Aufklärung*, that his Apollonian rationality loses all vitality and becomes decadence. *The Birth of Tragedy*'s criterion for condemning Socratism is not truth, but life. Socratic self-consciousness is "critiqued" and unmasked not because it is non-true, but because it is non-vital. This prefigures several complex developments in Nietzsche's subsequent unmasking of definite forms, of values, and of the very notion of truth. The suspicion aroused by self-conscious subjectivity is certainly inspired by the discovery that the forms which fed it, previously considered stable and definite, are actually false, being no more than sublimating appearances designed to comfort. However, these forms are unmasked and condemned not only for this, but also because, much like Socratic enlightened rationalism, they aspire to truth, forgetting that as deceptions they are bound to life, to the Dionysian. The complexity of this perspective will be found, expressed differently, in Nietzsche's subsequent work. Yet already in *The Birth of Tragedy* we find that he cannot stop with the unmasking of superficiality, of non-truth, of the self-consciousness of the subject: he must go on, advancing toward nihilism and the dissolution of the very notions of truth and being.

In the works that follow, beginning with the *Untimely Meditations* and *Human, All Too Human*, the unmasking of the superficiality of the self-conscious subject will in fact develop side by side with the unmasking of the notion of truth and with the broader dissolution of being as foundation. One can in fact say that the most representative expression of the crisis of subjectivity in Nietzsche is the announcement that "God is dead," which is formulated for the first time in *The Gay Science* and can be used as the emblematic utterance of Nietzsche's whole itinerary after his text on tragedy.

Nietzsche's radical unmasking of the superficiality of the *I* proceeds mainly through the awareness of the interplay of forces in social relations, especially power relations. The unpublished text "On Truth and Lying in an Extra-Moral Sense" shows how the world of truth and logic is constructed on the basis of an "obligation to deceive according to rules," socially determined and according to a system of metaphors warranted and legitimized by society. At the same time, all other metaphoric systems which herald creativity in the individual, if not relegated to the unconscious, are demoted to poetic fictions. *Human, Too Human* will conduct its entire critique of knowledge with similar arguments, insisting also on the fact that what we consider conscious experience is whatever we have a language for, names and possibilities of description in a socially convened and imposed model language. The world of consciousness will therefore tend to attain the configuration of a world of awarenesses shared by society and imposed on us via the conditioning that language requires. But there is more. The contents of our consciousness that concern the phenomenal world are not the only "fictions" regulated by social conventions. The image the *I* has of itself, in short, self-consciousness in its true sense, is now seen as the image of ourselves which others communicate to us and which we accept and adopt for reasons of security. To defend ourselves we must in fact introject others' perceptions of us, making our calculations accordingly. In the struggle for survival, mimicry, camouflage (*mimetismo*) is a crucial instrument). That which we call egoism is therefore only an "apparent egoism," as the title of aphorism 105 in *Daybreak* says explicitly:

> *Pseudo-egoism.* Whatever they may think and say about their "egoism," the great majority nonetheless do nothing for their ego their whole life long: what they do is done for the phantom of their ego which has formed itself in the heads of those around them and has been communicated to them; . . . all of them dwell in a fog of impersonal, semi-personal opinions . . . all these people, unknown to themselves, believe in the bloodless abstraction "man," that is to say, in a fiction. (Hollingdale trans.)

This fiction is precisely the result of these impersonal, diffuse, and all-pervading opinions which go on developing independently from the lives of individuals. The "social phantom" character of the ego has both linguistic and disciplinary roots. Linguistic because in order to communicate there's an obligation to deceive according to a system of socially accepted lies or metaphors. Disciplinary because the necessity to communicate our needs to others forces us to know and describe them in a systematic manner which is ultimately superficial. All of these exigencies seem to culminate in the relation between "those who command and those who obey," a relation which above all else requires self-consciousness.[8] If, on the one hand, the critique of the superficiality of consciousness and therefore of the subject in its most classical, metaphysical definition develops in the direction of the unmasking of its alleged immediacy and finality, and is brought back to the interplay of forces over which the subject has no control (being rather its result and expression). On the other hand, as it first appeared in the play between the Apollonian and the Dionysian in *The Birth of Tragedy* Nietzsche continues at the same time on the road toward the ever more explicit awareness of the "necessity of error" (cf.

Human, All Too Human, Part 1), a condition expressed in emblematic terms in aphorism 361 of *The Gay Science*, "The Problem of the Comedian," where we find an entire philosophy of culture as the production of "lies," systems of concepts and values that have no possibility of being "legitimated" vis-à-vis the true reality of things. These lawful deceits are borne by and multiply solely from the manifestation of a capacity to lie and to mask oneself which, though in origin an instrument of defense and survival, is now autonomous and develops beyond any possible vital function. Thus lying, metaphor, the inventiveness of culture creating worlds of appearances cannot any longer legitimize itself in terms of foundation, not even with the perspective of a vitalistic pragmatism. The discovery of lying, or of "dreaming" (as Nietzsche says in aphorism 54 of *The Gay Science* does not mean that we can stop lying and dreaming, but only that we must continue *dreaming while knowing* that we are dreaming: only in this fashion can we avoid perishing.

The whirlwind circularity of the conclusion of aphorism 54 in *The Gay Science* locates, in its broadest implications, the terms of the "crisis of subjectivity" the way Nietzsche discovered it and lived it: once unmasked, the superficiality of consciousness does not become the path to a new, more secure foundation. The non-finality of consciousness means, on the other hand, the end of *any* finality (*ultimità*), the impossibility, therefore, of thinking in terms of a foundation, and from that the general need to make adjustments in the definition of truth and of being. This broadening of the unmasking discourse to its most radical and vast ontological terms is actually the direction Nietzsche's mature works take, from *Zarathustra* onward. This period is marked by the discovery of the idea of the eternal recurrence of the same, of nihilism, of the will to power and the overman. All these terms define, much more than a positive, Nietzschean philosophy, his own ever problematic effort to realize an ontology after the end of foundational thinking, after the death of God. As far as the problem of subjectivity is concerned, the term with which Nietzsche defines his vision of a humanity no longer "subject(ed)" (in all its meanings and correlations, from subjectivity to subjugation) is that of *Übermensch, superman (superuomo)*, or, better, *overman (oltreuomo)*.[9] The problem with the notion of the overman consists in the fact that its most typical reading seems to lead to the position of metaphysical subjectivity-self-consciousness, self-control, will to power against others-and, what's more, a subjectivity that strengthens its more traditional aspects. Yet in the philosophy of eternal recurrence, in which "there are no facts, only interpretations,"[10] even the idea that there could only be interpreters—"is only an interpretation":

> Everything is subjective, you say; but this is already an *interpretation*, the "subject" is not a given, it is only something added through the imagination, something stuck on *afterwards*. Is it finally necessary to place the interpreter behind the interpretation? But this is already invention, hypothesis.[11]

If it is difficult to establish what or who is the overman, one thing is certain: it is not a strengthened *form* of metaphysical subjectivity, at least not in the sense of self-consciousness and will. In fact even will itself, which does nevertheless play such a central role in the later Nietzsche, is taken within the interplay of negation and de-founding (*sfondamento*) according to which everything is interpretation, even this very thesis. Within this context, what appears to give a positive—though problematic—characterization to man no longer subject, is *his* capacity to negate himself as subject, to go beyond all imperatives of self-preservation in the direction of limitless experimentation. This suggests, to some extent, the Schopenhauerian version of Kant's aesthetic disinterest, though radicalized even more. Ascetic ideals and all the complex, cruel games that moral and metaphysical man has played and dealt himself—and which today are further developed by the mindless hubris of technicians and engineers[12]—all seem to attest to the fact that with man there came upon the earth an unprecedented phenomenon, an animal capable of turning against himself, against his own spirit of self-preservation:

> the existence on earth of an animal soul turned against itself, taking sides against itself, was something so new, profound, unheard of, enigmatic, contradictory, *and pregnant with a future* that the aspect of the earth was essentially altered.[13]

The capacity to experiment beyond the interests of conservation is realized, according to Nietzsche, in the mindless or casual (*spensierata*) inventiveness of the technicians and the engineers—which makes one think that science and technology have a decisive role in defining man's new position, no longer subject, in the world. But these are fleeting remarks. For

Nietzsche, the exemplary figure of the overman is, in a fundamental sense, the artist. The ultrahuman path of art which he sketches in his last writings seems to point to the two main roads traveled by the avant-gardes of the twentieth century: on the one hand, the will to forms, the most radical technical experimentation conceivable; and on the other the dissolution of any rule of form in the name of an art no longer subjected to constructive ideals, but rather well on its way to the extreme experience of destructuration, toward the end of any hierarchy within the product as well as of the artist or consumer as subjects.

The open-ended problematic in which the figure of the overman remains does not only, or primarily, indicate a theoretical inconclusiveness or even an aporia that may characterize Nietzsche's thought. In expanding to a general ontological discourse that beckons the dissolution of being as foundation, this problematic alludes to the impossibility of redefining subjectivity by means of a simple theoretical design, with a clarification of concepts or a taking hold of errors. Metaphysics, Heidegger claims, is not merely an error we can escape, an opinion we can discard once we recognize its falsity.[14] Thus the collapse or untenability (*insostenibilità*) of the notion of subjectivity reflects the collapse of subjectivity itself in the world, in the present epoch of being: It cannot find a pacifying theoretical resolution at the hands of some clever thinker.

    The same itinerary that stretches from the unmasking of the metaphysical subject to the dissolution of being as foundation and to nihilism can also be employed to characterize Heidegger's meditation, though in different terms. Here again I must proceed sketchily, referring the reader to my more extensive treatments of the topic.[15] Guided loosely by the analogy with Nietzsche, one might say that what we can call the "unmasking" (*smascheramento*) of the subject in Heidegger's thought is the critique of the conceptions of man as a *Vorhandenes*, a "thing" among many other things characterized solely by specific attributes. For example, Heidegger mentions in his text on Humanism the metaphysical definition of man as a member of the animal genus endowed with reason as its specific difference. In *Being and Time* man is not thinkable as a subject precisely because this would make him something "merely present." Man is, instead, the *Dasein*, being-there (*l'esserci*) that is, above all, projection. For Heidegger, the subject is characterized by a substantiality which is no longer present in Dasein as project: man is defined not as a given determinate substance, but as a "having-to-be," an opening upon possibility. Dasein thinks of itself as subject, that is, as substance, only when it thinks itself inauthentically, with the horizon of the public and everyday *they*.[16]

The definition of Dasein in terms of projection rather than in terms of subjectivity does not, however, evidence the character of an unmasking which leads to a new and more satisfying (and reassuring) foundation. To say that Dasein is projection opens up, in fact, the question of authenticity, which is central to *Sein und Zeit* and, in different terms, throughout Heidegger's subsequent development. Since the project cannot be made authentic by referring to any sort of pregiven substantiality—for example, a nature, or an essence, etc.—it can only achieve authenticity by choosing the possibility which is most proper, but not in the sense of appropriate (which legitimates by referring to a basic structure or substance), but in the sense of being unavoidable and ever open as possibility which, as long as *Dasein* is, remains such. This "most proper" possibility is the impending possibility of death. The project which is *Dasein* is authentically chosen only as it decides ahead of time with regards to its own death. As is well known, Heidegger refuses to describe in existential terms the meaning of this anticipatory decision. It does not obviously correspond to the decision to put an end to one's life by means of suicide, nor does it entail a "thinking about death" in terms of the Christian warning about becoming dust.[17] The content couched in the notion of the anticipatory decision concerning death is rather to be sought in those pages of the second section of *Being and Time*—those pages which open up with the problematic of being-towards-death-where Heidegger speaks of our historical heritage. (See especially par. 74 and moreover in those pages where he speaks of the relationship of Dasein with others, in par. 53.) The meaning of these pages can be gathered by reading a passage from a much later work, *Der Satz vom Grund*, in which Heidegger no longer speaks of authenticity or inauthenticity.[18] These terms and problems are now channeled, and transformed, in the new thematic of the eventuality of being. The shift can be best understood if we bear in mind the terminology of the original German: authentic is *eigentlich*; the event is now understood as *Ereignis*. What they both have in common is the root, *eigen*, which means *proper*. In this passage, what in *Being and Time* was the anticipatory decision concerning death now becomes the "leap" in the abyss of the "liberating tie with tradition" (ibid., 187). The tradition of which Heidegger speaks in *Der Satz vom Grund* is not what in *Being and Time* is called *tradition*, which was characterized as an acceptance of the past as both dead and irrevocable (therefore anything but liberating). Within tradition the past is conceived as *vergangen* (gone, past), and this represents the mode according to which inauthentic experience is related to the past. True authentic existence thinks the past, instead, as *gewesen*—not as past, dead and irrevocable, but as "having been"—and its tradition is now called *Über-lieferung*, with the German root word meaning *überliefern*, that is, *transmitting*. If we now turn to *Being and Time* for the difference between *Tradition* and *Überlieferung*, between accepting the past as *vergangen* and the capacity to hand it down as *gewesen*, we find that in the latter case the past is accepted within the perspective of the anticipatory decision of death. Only by projecting itself in anticipation of one's own death can Being see the past as history, as a heritage of yet open possibilities which speak as models of possibility as well as possible models. The authentic relationship with the past is opened up by the awareness of one's own mortality, a condition that assumes as only mortal even the traces and the models which have been handed down through history. The leap into the *Überlieferung* is a liberating move because it removes us from the order of the "given," that is, from what is inherited (and within which the project of *Dasein* finds itself thrown), or the finality of a "natural order." The leap into the *Überlieferung* is (only) event, only trace of other possible-mortal existences which *Dasein* accepts or rejects as possibilities still open to it.[19]

What we are dealing with is a topic which seems very far from Nietzsche's. The similarity and the parallels which, in this light, exist between the Nietzschean and the Heideggerian itineraries will appear less problematic if we think for a moment that here, also, as with Nietzsche, what takes place during the meditation upon the limits and the untenability of the notion of subjectivity is the discovery of the groundlessness of being. The discourse on the possible authenticity of *Dasein* deals in fact with Being itself, and it is no mere accident that in Heidegger's later writings this discourse opens up to being as event. The question of authenticity is not purely a problem of an "ethical" or "psychological" aspect of that particular being (i.e., entity) called *Dasein*. Already in *Being and Time* things, objects, the world in its wholeness come to being, or give themselves as entities, only insofar as there's being-there, *Dasein* which opens up the horizon of their givenness. Therefore there's no being outside, or before, or independently of the thrown project which *Dasein* is. That this project can realize itself as authentic only as it decides concerning its own death—that is to say, in the form of the liberating bond with tradition, in assuming the historical heritage as *gewesen,* possibility, having-been-mortality—all this means (with the help of passages which we cannot reconstruct here in analytic fashion but which are certainly understandable to the reader of Heidegger's last writings), that being is Event, that being *is-not,* but rather "happens," discloses itself.

Within the framework of our guiding hypothesis, this is also what we can call Heidegger's nihilism. Like Nietzsche, Heidegger expands the collapse of metaphysical subjectivity into a general ontological discourse which experiences the "de-grounding" (*s-fondamento*) of being by discovering the constitutive relationship between existence and death. Existence appropriates and becomes authentic (*eigentlich*) only as it lets itself be expropriated, deciding towards its own death in the event (*Ereignis*) which is both expropriating and transpropriating (*enteignend* and *übereignend*). This is being itself as *Überlieferung,* transmission of traces, messages, linguistic formations in which alone our experience of the world is rendered possible, and in which things come to being.

This breaking-through or de-grounding towards ontology—a nihilistic ontology, to be sure, and another trait that links Nietzsche and Heidegger—takes place, as hinted above, not as the result of a pure shifting of concepts, but in relation to more general transformations in the conditions of existence which have to do with modern technology and its rationalization in today's world. In Nietzsche, the line of reasoning is very straightforward: the death of God means the end of belief in ultimate values and foundation, because these beliefs corresponded to the need for reassurance typical of a humanity somehow still primitive. The rationalization and organization of social work and the development of science and technology which have been made possible precisely by the religious-metaphysical vision of the world (we can think of the sociology of religion in Max Weber and the relationship he established between capitalistic science-technology and Judeo-Christian monotheism) have rendered these beliefs superfluous. This is, incidentally, another way of conceiving nihilism. The destiny of subjectivity unveiled in its groundlessness, and the nihilistic dissolution of being are thus inextricably bound up with each other and with the history of the technics-scientific rationalization of the world. It is precisely the technical organization of the world that makes obsolete both being as foundation and the hierarchic, dominated structure of self-consciousness or subjectivity.

In Heidegger the passage from the level of the existential analytic (in *Being and Time*) to that of the history of metaphysics as the history of being—which corresponds to the turn in his thought beginning in the 1930s—takes place precisely in reference to the awareness that, in a world like ours and his, made up of great historical powers which tend to be totalizing and totalitarian, the essence of man cannot (any longer, if it ever could) think itself in terms of individual structures, or in terms of suprahistorical definitions. It should not be difficult to show, if we bear in mind those historically more compromised and compromising pages of the *Introduction to Metaphysics* (the 1935 course in which Heidegger addresses explicitly the question of the destiny of the West, of Germany, Russia, and America, and their tendency to institute themselves as systems of total domination),[20] that the explication of the verbal as opposed to the nominal sense of essence—*Wesen*, read as a verb in the infinitive: *to become an essence* (*essenzializzarsi*), to determine—manifests itself each and every time in a destiny-like manner, in an epochal fashion. Moreover, to happen (*accadere*) is linked both to the awareness of the weight that historical superpowers possess in determining the destiny of humanity, and to the givenness of those "thrown" projections which make up, each and every time, time and again, the disclosures of the truth of being in which historical humanities (the historical-destinal essences of man) define themselves. Now this weight that leads being to give-itself—to make itself known and happen, take place in its epochality and to become event—unveils itself precisely in the modern world of science-and-technology. This is not, once again, an eternal structure which would in the end become visible only to ourselves—it is rather the epochal happening (coming-to-being) of being within the framework of the conditions that can be verified with the technological organization of the world, which is "tendentially" totalizing. Heidegger will express all of this much later in certain passages of *Identity and Difference*, in which he will speak of the *Ge-Stell* (which I suggested be translated, at least in Italian, as *im-posizione* [literally: im-position]),[21] that is, of the system of total organization typical of the techno-scientific view of the world, as the fulfillment of metaphysics and as the "first flash" of the event of being, in short, as a *chance* to go beyond metaphysics made possible by the fact that in the *Gestell* man and being lose those very characteristics which metaphysics had attributed to them—above all, their position or status as subject and object.[22]

Beyond *the* Subject?

It would be yet another metaphysical illusion—implicitly tied to the idea that there could be an ordered world of essences—to think that we can extract a lesson from Nietzsche and Heidegger on the true nature of subjectivity such that we may correct our errors concerning this specific *topos* of philosophy. What we have found, instead, is that the untenability, the internal contradictoriness of the metaphysical conception of the subject (in Nietzsche the discovery of its superficiality and its non-finality; in Heidegger the experience of the groundless projection) is given only as the collapse of the subject itself in a world radically transformed by the techno-scientific organization and which brings to its limit, explicitly for Heidegger and implicitly for Nietzsche, the notion of metaphysics as the thought of foundations. The "beyonding of the metaphysical conception of the subject is, within this perspective, a going beyond the historical-destinal "essences" of metaphysical subjectivity, and this involves the problem of the surpassing of metaphysics in its concrete-historical givenness, as the world of total organization. In short, the fact that Nietzsche's overman and Heidegger's "re-calling" thought are not so clearly defined as alternative solutions to the crisis of metaphysical subjectivity should not be taken as a limit or incapacity on the part of either of the two thinkers, but must be understood as evidence of a "destining" condition—more specifically, in the Heideggerian sense of *Geschick*, which alludes to a "sending" a heritage which calls forth as possibility, and not as a deterministically fixed fate conceivable only within the horizon of necessitating metaphysical structures. Since the experience of the *Ge-Stell* or of the death of God as announced by Nietzsche places us in front of the historic-destining of the *Wesen*, the coming to pass of being: we should not search for guiding threads, pointers, or legitimations in suprahistorical structures, but ought rather to look only at the *Geschick*, at the ensemble of meanings which, by taking the risk of interpretation (which can be authentic only if it projects itself towards death, if it takes the responsibility of its radical groundlessness), we can succeed in recognizing in the taking place (*accadere*) into which we are thrown.

In different ways but following similar motivations, Nietzsche and Heidegger tell us that this happening be defined as *Gestell*, as the world of science-and-technology; moreover, in this world we must search for the traits of a post-metaphysical humanity which is no longer "subject(ed)" ("*soggetta*").

But is not the world of science-and-technology, also the world of totalitarian organization, the world of dehumanization, the world of planning that reduces every humanity, every individual experience, every personal expression to a moment of a statistically foreseeable normality—and when it doesn't fall within this middling capacity—to an accidental marginality devoid of consequence? Nietzsche and Heidegger seem to bet, each in his own way, on yet another possibility, though this also is tied to the unfolding of modem science-and-technology. For Nietzsche, the world in which God is dead because the organization of social work has rendered superfluous that excessive reassurance that it represented, is also the world in which reality becomes lighter, in that it becomes possible to "dream knowing one is dreaming," and in which, finally, life can carry on within less dogmatic horizons, contexts that are less violent and at the same time explicitly dialogical, experimental, risky. It is true that for Nietzsche this perspective is fundamentally open only to artists, or at any rate only to a sector of humankind, since the majority of people, according to him, remain bound to providing, by means of planned manual labor, the very freedom of these few. But this is probably the aspect of his philosophy which we can define still as "modern," against the more explicit "postmodernity" of Heidegger. It is likely, in fact, that the elitist and aesthetic conception of the overman on Nietzsche's part is secretly linked to an image of the world of science-and-technology which is fundamentally machinistic (*macchinica*), an idea, that is, according to which technology consists above all in the invention of machines in order to multiply the physical strength of man and increase his capacity of "mechanical" domination (as in moving, relocating, transporting, etc.) over nature. This conception of technology has as its paradigmatic model the motor or the engine. To the degree in which the capacity of the motor is seen as the capacity to channel and utilize energy to induce modifications and physical alterations in nature and matter, the overcoming of subjectivity which such a technology allows coincides with the overcoming of the subjection to manual labor. Yet this remains the fundamental model of any type of labor in a world whose development is conceived solely as an ever growing multiplication of the capacity to "move" (*spostare*), to utilize energy in a mechanical sense.

Nevertheless, we can hold on to Heidegger's conception of technology as being modelled more or less explicitly upon information theory or telematics (*telematica*), which constitutes the essence of latemodern or postmodern technology. The *Gestell* does not entail the possibility for man to dispose of his metaphysical traits as subject because, in the technological world, he becomes factory worker, part and parcel with the machine. More radically, instead, information technology seems to render subjectivity unthinkable for it is not given to one subject to possess or to manipulate, within a logic still bound to a master-slave metaphysics, the information from whose coordination and connections depend the true power of the latemodern world. We are not talking here of the negative utopia of the robots that would take over the world; rather, we are more realistically taking cognizance of the intensification of social complexity, which is not simplified but is rendered more diffuse and pervasive by means of the technology that goes with information. This renders the conceiving of humanity in terms of multiple subjective poles, characterized by self-consciousness and by spheres of conflictual power—rather impossible. Only on this account, perhaps, can the Nietzschean and the Heideggerian meditation on the destiny of subjectivity in the epoch of the dissolution of being as foundation contain for us some indications pregnant with a future.

Appendix 2

Hermeneutics as *Koine*

What is the meaning of the thesis according to which hermeneutics is the *koine* of philosophy and, more generally, of culture in the 1980s? The claim, which can be reasonably argued, is that in much the same way in which we witnessed in the past decades a Marxist hegemony (in the 1950s and the 1960s) and a structuralist hegemony (in the 1970s, generalizing somewhat), today the common idiom of both philosophy and culture is hermeneutics. Obviously we do not intend to prove that in the decades just referred to there was a Marxist and then a structuralist hegemony, nor that today there exists a hermeneutic hegemony. The claim concerning hermeneutics as *koine* holds that, from the viewpoint of factual description, similarly to the way in which in the past the great majority of literary and philosophical discussions had to rise to the challenge of Marxism and structuralism, often without necessarily accepting any of their tenets, today this central role belongs to hermeneutics.

At the time when Gadamer first published *Truth and Method* (1960), hermeneutics was no more than a technical term indicating, for culture at large, a very specialized discipline that dealt with the interpretation of literary, juridical, and theological texts. As has often happened with other expressions, like "philosophy of language," which for a while stood to signify analytic philosophy tout court, today the term "hermeneutics" has acquired a broader philosophical meaning that denotes both a specific philosophical discipline and a theoretical orientation, a "current." With reference to either or both of these meanings (and with a certain, inevitable, ambiguity), the centrality of hermeneutics and its connected themes and texts is attested by the presence of the term in cultural discussions, education, university courses, and even in those areas such as medicine, sociology, architecture, to name just a few, which are presently seeking new links with philosophy.

Vague as it may sound, all this adds up to ascertaining the increased popularity of hermeneutics in today's culture. Yet the claim becomes less generic the moment we start looking for the plausible reasons behind this timeliness (*attualità*) of hermeneutics. The search for these reasons constitutes a first step toward a clearer understanding of the initial thesis. We shall ask ourselves what it means, and what needs and transformations are articulated by the fact—if that's what it is—that hermeneutics is enjoying such popularity. This first question—What is articulated in the relevance of hermeneutics?—spurs a second one: In what direction and toward what end is the interest in hermeneutics pointing? Both questions and their respective answers are theoretically relevant to the contents and development of hermeneutics itself. The fact that it has become, if not altogether hegemonic then at least a common idiom, means that hermeneutics today is faced with problems and tasks which are new and different with respect to those that were pertinent to the Gadamerian project of 1960. Confronted with new questions and tasks, it is likely that hermeneutics must redefine itself, and attempt to circumscribe the indefiniteness that characterizes it precisely insofar as it is a *koine*. For example, in the last few years in America, hermeneutics has come to represent more or less all of continental European philosophy, that is to say what not too long ago, in the same cultural environment, was called phenomenology or existentialism. Today in fact hermeneuticians are not only Gadamer and Ricoeur, but Derrida, Foucault, Apel, and Habermas as well. The question therefore remains: If hermeneutics has become the cultural *koine* of the past few years, to what do we owe this state of affairs?

A preliminary answer to the question might be formulated as follows: hermeneutics is the form in which, with the waning of the structuralist hegemony, a historicist exigency is once again demanding to be heard. It is in fact unlikely that the crisis and dissolution of structuralism is to be imputed solely to the exhaustion of a critical fad—that is to say, that at a given point in time the structural method was reduced to a caricature of itself for having imposed on all the human sciences rigid patterns of description and cataloguing. Grounded upon binary oppositions, these critical grids favored the pure and simple possibility of discovering ordering principles; even certain exaggerated claims made by microhistory reflect this extremely formalistic cultural climate in which everything appeared to be worthy of investigation as long as it exhibited some structuring principle. But if the runaway proliferation of descriptive schemes—more or less an end in themselves—contributed in no uncertain way to the dissolution of the structuralist hegemony (owing precisely to its excessive radicalization), the crisis of structuralism has even deeper roots. Brought to its ultimate consequences, structural method reduced content to its inessentiality because it placed in a position of abstract and never thematized neutrality the "deploying" subject of the method itself. The contents to which the method was applied—the comic strip, the feuilleton, the history of smell and so on—were considered irrelevant to the degree in which the interest of the observer was considered purely cognitive. But it was precisely this purity and cognitive aspect that needed to be questioned. It is true that the structuralists rightly appealed to the political significance of wanting to study people as if they were ants (following Lévi-Strauss in polemic with Sartre the humanist) against a historicist and evolutionistic tradition that made of the West the center of the world and easily justified the ideology of imperialism. Indeed structuralism has also been, since 1968, one of the theoretical weapons of the left, with the theory of decolonization, partaking in the effort to give other cultures the right to speak. Yet all of this came about, as we perceive today, at the cost of a positivistic restoration of the presupposed neutrality of the observer. Perhaps that was, ultimately, the sense of Althusser's oxymoron "theoretical practice."

Within the scope of these broad generalizations concerning the sociology of culture, it is likely that the exhaustion of the structuralist fad corresponds moreover to a new phase in the relation between Western culture and other cultures. Today, when for better or for worse these other cultures have gained the right to speak—above all the Islamic culture, with its pressure, political and otherwise, on the West—we can no longer ignore the problem of the relation between the observer and the observed. The dialogue with different cultures has finally become a true dialogue. And it is pointless to liquidate the Eurocentric perspectives that structuralism in years past rightfully meant to defuse. The question today is rather to truly exercise this dialogue beyond a purely descriptive position.

Without meaning to overstate these rather approximative observations, we can call to mind, among the signs of this passage from a structuralist *koine* to a hermeneutic *koine*, certain representative vicissitudes of the semiotic work of Umberto Eco. During the past few years, Eco has in fact shown an increased interest in the pragmatic aspects of semiotics, shifting in the meantime the emphasis from Saussure to Peirce, with all that this entails. On the same scale we can perceive the itinerary of a thinker who, though he identified himself as a structuralist, has greatly influenced the newer definition of structuralist themes and their mode of interaction in culture, namely Jacques Derrida. As Maurizio Ferraris (1984) pointed out, Derrida's more recent works are marked by a growing interest in the institutional collocation of the philosopher and in general by the "conflict of faculties," in other words, by the pragmatic and historical-concrete aspects of metaphysics and its deconstruction.

These facts seem to indicate that the crisis of the structuralist *koine* is motivated by demands that are by and large historicist. It is these exigencies that explain the shift, the passage to hermeneutics, its coming onto the scene as the most likely candidate to represent the cultural *koine* of the 1980s. But how does hermeneutics perceive, more than structuralism ever did, this exigency to reassign an essential aspect to contents and thematize the historical position of the observer?

We are now faced with the second question concerning the timeliness (*attualità*) of hermeneutics. At this juncture, I wish to discuss not only if and to what extent hermeneutics can validate its claim to the essentiality of historical collocation, but also try to demonstrate that, in order to understand these exigencies, hermeneutics must redefine itself in a more rigorous and coherent manner by recovering its original inspiration, that is, the Heideggerian meditation on metaphysics and its destiny. In general, the fact that thinking turns to hermeneutics in order to retrieve the historicity and essentiality of contents that structuralism had forgotten is legitimated by the determining importance that interpretation theory in Gadamer's classic formulation, attributes to the *Wirkungsgeschichte* (effective history) and the *Wirkungsgeschichtliches Bewusstsein* (effective-historical consciousness). Interpretation is not description on the part of a neutral observer, rather, it is a dialogic event in which the interlocutors are equally played out and from which their result changed in some way. They understand one another being situated within a third horizon, a horizon they do not have any control over but within which and by which they are placed (*dentro un orizzonte terzo, di cui non dispongono, ma nel quale e dal quale sono disposti*). Whereas structural thinking had as its *telos* the evidencing and taking possession of, on the part of the observing consciousness, orders linked according to rules, hermeneutic thinking emphasizes the fact that both observer and observed belong together within a common horizon, underscoring truth as an event that, in the dialogue between the two interlocutors, "realizes" or "sets into play" (*mette in opera*) and modifies at the same time this horizon. In the context of play, which in *Truth and Method* Gadamer takes as the model for the disclosure of hermeneutic truth, the players are also and always being played; thus consciousness, insofar as it is historically determined, cannot ever reach total self-transparency.

Reformulated in this fashion, hermeneutics retrieves and develops the heritage of existentialism's critique of Hegel's metaphysical rationalism, as well as existentialism's critique of that positivistic scientism which in some ways is still echoed by structuralism. If the above hypotheses are valid, the political-concrete-historical distress experienced by thinking when the effective historical collocation of the observer is not accounted for is really not too different from the existentialist critique of idealism and positivism. Phenomenologically ascertained lived experience of thought refuses to accept philosophical schemes that presuppose an observing subject as a neutral point of view, or, which amounts to the same thing, as an opacity that clarifies itself until it reaches the absolute self-transparency of the Hegelian spirit. Against the alleged (at times implicitly) positivistic and structural neutrality, hermeneutics vindicates the fact that the subject belongs to the play necessary to comprehension and to the event of truth. However, instead of seeing this play as process motivated by the *telos* of self-transparency (Hegel), hermeneutics considers the belonging, the playing while being played, as a definitive phase that cannot be overcome in a final moment of appropriation and fruition of the subject's presuppositions.

In what sense is the "fusion of horizons," the reciprocal understanding of the two interlocutors in the "objective spirit," an event of truth for Gadamer? In an essay that is important to understand the significance Gadamer himself attributes to his thought within contemporary philosophy—"The Philosophical Foundations of the Twentieth Century" (1973)—he states that today philosophy should seek for its guide the Hegelian notions of objective spirit. The total mediation which Hegel conceived as the task and supreme *telos* of thought does not take place in the self-consciousness of absolute spirit—a monologic self-consciousness that is still understood as the consciousness of a Cartesian ego—but rather in objective spirit, that is to say, in culture, institutions, the symbolic forms that make up the substance of our lived humanness. Here we can take almost literally Lacan's reading of Freud: not "*no Es war, soll ich werden,*" but "*wo Es ar, soll ich warden.*" Truth is experienced solely by advancing to where the concreteness of objective spirit is given, not by dissolving this concreteness in a fully displayed self-consciousness. The ethical-political perspective Gadamer has worked in recent writings on the basis of premises present already in *Truth and Method* (1960), for instance, in *Reason in the Age of Science* (1976), illustrates the meaning he attributes to this choice for a Hegelian objective spirit. For the task of thinking consists in bringing everything, and above all the results of specialistic approaches to reality, as well as the formalized languages of science and their technological applications, to face the *logos* that dwells in the tradition of language, to what Habermas in his more recent writings calls "lifeworld" (with a term that, though Husserlian in the letter, is substantially hermeneutic).

But why, one might still ask, does the hermeneutic experience of truth take the shape of a "moving toward the objective spirit"? Are we dealing with that abdication to the overpowering object for which Adorno (1966) reproached Heidegger in the chapter on "Ontological Need" in *Negative Dialectics*? Gadamer, however, is not so much a traditionalist (for whom truth is what adapts to common sense, the cultural patrimony actually inherited by a society, that which is handed down), as he is a classicist: the experience of truth is for him an experience of integration, of nonconflictual belonging. Crucial to this are the pages he devotes to the notion of the beautiful, the *kalòn* of the Greeks, in both already cited works.

It is legitimate to call such a position classicist to the degree to which it recovers the seventeenth- and eighteenth-century dream of a Greek experience understood as the full correspondence between internal and external, between human being and citizen: the same that is perceived in Hegel's notion of "beautiful ethicalness" and his conception of classical art. But does this conception of truth as a classically modelled belonging really respond to that need for historicalness that hermeneutics as a post-historicist, poststructuralist *koine* is called upon to satisfy? Isn't there perhaps a danger that the experience of truth as *kalòn* (nonconflictual belonging of the interlocutors among themselves and with respect to the horizon of language, of objective spirit, and of living tradition that mediates them) is just another way in which the transparent, ahistorical, neutralized subject manifests itself? It is a legitimate doubt if we think for a moment of the apparent inconclusiveness that hermeneutics seems to manifest, though not so much in Gadamer's own work as in its current public image. For the Gadamer of *Truth and Method* (1960), it was a question of vindicating the legitimacy of an "extra-methodic" experience of truth: the truth of art, the truth of history, the truth of tradition living in language, as well as the constitutive linguisticalness of experience. Gadamer successfully achieved these goals, but as a result of this, and with the present preeminence of hermeneutics as *koine*, it becomes clear that hermeneutics cannot stop here. It is a question neither of vindicating a classicistic model of truth against the objectivism of scientific method erected as sole arbiter of the true, nor of acknowledging that there exists an "extra-methodic" truth side by side with scientific truth.

Ultimately, it is not a question of substituting a hermeneutic description of experience with one that is realistic or objectivistic. Perhaps it is true that a philosophy cannot become a *koiné* without realizing itself as an emancipatory program. From this point of view, Habermas' objections to Gadamer were right on target (though its results were unacceptable because tied to a revival of Kantianism and therefore in favor of an ahistorical subjectivity (see Vattimo, 1981). However, it is also true that to require an emancipatory perspective is theoretically outside the scope of hermeneutics. Yet, by the same token one cannot demand of philosophical hermeneutics that it limit itself to yet another description of the structures of experience. By holding that truth is not exclusively the proposition that describes faithfully from the outside a state of affairs, but rather it is constituted of events, responses, and messages that hail from a tradition and stand as new messages communicated to other interlocutors, hermeneutics cannot but engage concretely in responding to its own tradition and in opening up the dialogue to other traditions with which it comes into contact. Hermeneutics cannot be only a theory of dialogue; as a matter of fact, perhaps it cannot think of itself as a theory of dialogue at all (if the latter is understood as the true structure of any human experience, which in its universal essence would still have to be described metaphysically). Rather, if it intends to be coherent with its own premises, hermeneutics must *articulate* itself *as* dialogue, thus committing itself concretely vis-à-vis the contents of tradition. Here the external exigency that demands of hermeneutics an emancipatory perspective meets up with the internal exigency of "coherence" and consequence of the discipline itself.

In the end, is a theory of dialogue enough? Will a description of experience as continuity, an appeal to bring experience to bear on the stratified wealth of our tradition, therefore a certain classicism in the most literal and historical sense of the term, suffice? Will an emphasis—which is what in the last analysis we find in Habermas's "Theory of Communicative Action" (1984)—on tolerance, on argumentative exchange, on reason as reasonableness and persuasion exercised in social dialogue be enough? But, in a dialogue, we do have—insofar as we are hermeneuticians who do not wish to be solely transcendental philosophers—something to say. And what is it that we want to say besides the fact that we talk about dialogue as the only possible place for the event of truth?

Confronted with questions that surface the moment it becomes a *koine*, hermeneutics ought to reconsider its foundations, and more pointedly its Heideggerian heritage. In the wake of Gadamer's "urbanization" (Habermas's observation) of Heidegger, what has been partially lost (or at least pushed in the background) is Heidegger's conception of metaphysics as history of being. As is well known, Gadamer does not endorse Heidegger's verdict against Greek metaphysics. In the light of a phenomenology of lived experience that is, by the way, highly problematic from the hermeneutic perspective (as it is guided by the idea that we can reach the things in themselves and not only the transmitted words), Gadamer holds that what needs to be critiqued is the consignment of truth to the ambit of scientific-positive method, a reduction that took place between the eighteenth and nineteenth centuries (and in which Kantianism played a crucial role). On the basis of these premises, *Truth and Method* does not appear to be radical enough to grasp the situation of modern techno-scientific civilization. It is true that, on the ethic-political level, Gadamer appeals to the necessity of bringing specializations and sectorial finalities in contact with common awareness and its continuity with the tradition embodied in language, but this tradition runs the risk of appearing a bit overly humanistically stylized, as a (though respectable) "supplement of the soul."

If, on the other hand, and in line with Heidegger, we think of metaphysics as the history of being—which means above all that we grant an underlying unity between the two cultures, the humanistic and the scientific, as expressions of the same epoch of being, it is possible that hermeneutic thought succeeds in formulating a more radical emancipatory program, the consequence of a more explicit commitment to its proper historical collocation. The living continuity of tradition to which we must appeal in order to give a norm to science and technics and, more generally, to find the bearings for the problem of ethics, is precisely what Heidegger calls history of metaphysics or history of being. In this history what comes to the fore is not only the problem of recognizing, beyond (and more fundamentally than) the truth of science, the truth of art, history, and so on; this is certainly important, of course, but only as a moment in a more vast process which Heidegger places under the sign of the constitutive tendency of being to withdraw while revealing itself, that is to say, being as the ongoing happening of metaphysics until the moment in which, culminating in the Gestell (the universal technoscientific organization of the world), metaphysics comes to an end and its overcoming becomes possible.

It is with reference to this notion of history—and not, therefore, to a historicity which runs the constant risk of being broadly understood as belonging and dialogicalness—that hermeneutics historically commits itself and thinks its proper task in terms which are radically nontranscendental. If hermeneutics is not the discovery of the constitutive and objective dialogic-finite structure of each human experience, but rather a moment in the history of metaphysics as the history of being, both the problem of thinking oneself coherently as the interlocutor of a dialogue, as well as the related problem of defining oneself in terms of an emancipatory task (or: a historical task) take on different configurations. To say that hermeneutics is a decisive stage in the course through which being withdraws (even by literally dissolving) from the dominion of the metaphysical categories of fully displayed presence, is tantamount to saying that hermeneutic thought situates itself in a non-contemplative position, being rather engaged with respect to this course, supplying moreover guidance and criteria in order to make content choices.

To respond to the questions elicited by its new position as *koine* hermeneutics seems compelled to rediscover, paradoxically, the philosophy of history. I say paradoxically because the sense of this philosophy of history is nothing more than the (protracted) end of the philosophy of history. After all, even the modern philosophies of history are essential moments of that metaphysics which, according to Heidegger, can be overcome only in the form of the *Verwindung*, that is to say, in recovery-acceptance-distortion. Ricoeur too, by concentrating on 'time and narrative,' has perhaps captured this need to rethink historicalness, though once again he appears to have resolved it on the plane of a structural description instead of a radical conception of hermeneutics as a moment in the history of being. Outside of such a radicalization I cannot see other means by which hermeneutics can respond to the questions posed not only by philosophy but also by ever different and numerous fields of culture today.

Notes

Translator's Introduction

1. With this expression I will heretofore understand what has variously been called the Eurologocentric tradition, or the Hellenistic/Judeo-Christian cultural horizon. Like Heidegger, Vattimo is an epochal thinker, and his studies constantly hark to the most fundamental philosophical questions. All translations from the Italian are my own. I will incorporate sources of citations from Vattimo in my text by means of shortened title, year and page where appropriate.

2. Throughout these remarks, whenever I am not specifically glossing Vattimo's use of the term, I will use the word *interpretation* as an umbrella word which encompasses criticism, reviewing, interviews, scholarly studies, translations, in short, a panoply of ways which force the text (or cultural artifact) to touch and interact with a multifarious and elusive, indeed transparent, reality.

3. This applies to the heroic efforts of the well-known canonic, strong thinkers, the great systematizers, such as Kant, Hegel, Marx, as well as to the destroyers of the myth or dream of a reasoned coherent subject, such as Nietzsche, Heidegger, Derrida, Deleuze and Guattari, and Foucault.

4. For a detailed exposition of Vattimo's idea of nihilism, see in *La fine della modernità* the essays "apologia del nichilismo" and "Nichilismo e postmoderno in filosofia" (Vattimo 1975, 27–38 and 172–90). Eng. tr. J. Snyder. *The End of Modernity*. Baltimore: Johns Hopkins University Press, 1991.

5. See Vattimo 1987a and the commentary in Carravetta 1991a, 228–31.

6. Besides Ricouer, this primary dimension has been at the heart of the different hermeneutics of Habermas and Apel, which Vattimo never ceased to critique for their adoption of a modified transcendental subjectivity. On the need to look at Rhetorics with a hermeneutic spirit, and/or to address the rhetorical aspect of all hermeneutic enterprise, see the work of Calvin Schrag.

7. Though the early Vattimo is everywhere categorical about his rejection of Husserlian intentionality (seeing it as a development of Kantism and no longer

appealing after Heidegger's critique), throughout this book and later when he addresses broader social issues, the unavoidable admitting to or positing (even when merely giving an example) of a relating force, or thought, suggests that some form of intentionality or consciousness-of is allowed within the hermeneutic realm. The philosopher G. B. Madison, who may have more in common with Vattimo than meets the eye, had also warned against the dangers of phenomenology relying on a "transcendental subjectivism," but had also conceived of hermeneutics as "the interpretive activity of a thinking subject which turns back and reflects on itself in the aim of achieving a heightened self-understanding, is guided by what could be called the 'presupposition of meaning.'" (Madison 1990, 91). Significantly, Madison cites Ricoeur's early conjoining of phenomenology and hermeneutics, which contains the seed of his later work on time and narration: "It must be supposed that experience in all its fullness . . . has an expressibility (*dicibilité*) in principle. Experience *can* be said, it demands to be said. To bring it to language is not to change it into something else, but, in articulating and developing it, to make it become itself." It is clear how this resounds with much post-Heideggerian reflection on the relationship between language and being, and is fully theorized in H. G. Gadamer's *Truth and Method* (1975).

8. It is relevant to note, however, that Vattimo's dissertation, which he defended in 1957, dealt with *The Concept of "Making/Doing" in Aristotle*. This early acquisition of the role and range of rational or formal philosophizing may explain why throughout his career—even when critiquing instrumental and strong theorizing—he never veered toward anything resembling irrationalism or abstracting idealisms. Though he attacked the neo-rationalists of the early the 1980s when the landmark 1979 Gargani anthology *Crisi della ragione* (Crisis of Reason) came out (cf. Carravetta 1988), in *Oltre l'interpretazione* (Beyond Interpretation) (1994; Eng. trans. 1997) he dedicates a chapter to "The Reconstruction of Rationality."

9. For general overviews of the teeming activity that followed the forming of the new Republic, see various papers by Agazzi and Bobbio that fit this ideological profile. See also Carravetta 2014 for a reconstruction of the major trends following the end of the war.

10. Considering the counterforces of the twenty-two year experience of fascist dictatorship and the ravages of five years of war, Italy was certainly one of the miracle economies of the earlier cold war era, tracing an economic growth curve similar to that of West Germany, Israel, and Japan.

11. For historiographic reconstructions of Italian existentialism, see Santucci 1969 and Pareyson 1950.

12. The histories and historiographies of Italian Marxism vary widely, and it is not necessary here to specify any one preferred theory. For an overview, see the still useful De Grand 1989 and Bobbio 1990.

13. See various papers collected in Agazzi's 1989 anthology.

14. See Santucci 1969. Pareyson's interpretation of existentialism competed with those of Nicola Abbagnano, Enzo Paci, and Cesare Luporini.

15. For a synthesis and critique of two of the most important works by Pareyson, namely his *Estetica* (Esthetic) (1954) and *Verità e interpretazione* (*Truth and Interpretation*) (1970), see in English the introduction by Paolo Diego Bubbio to his translation of Pareyson, *Existence, Interpretation, Freedom: Selected Writings* (2009).

16. For the complex ways in which Heidegger was read, translated, and developed in Italy, see the rich gathering in Olivetti, 1989 (*The Italian reception of Heidegger*), 1989.

17. This is an assesment, an explanation of how things stood after Heidegger. Vattimo's next step, that of comprehension or interpretation, is worth citing since it contains the seeds of his later critique of Derrida: "This does not mean that there aren't philosophers who do metaphysics; but in this case they can only pick up yet again and repeat positions whose ultimate meaning is already cleared and has already been sucked in Nietzsche's philosophy" (Ibid. 23).

18. This was a delicate task, since besides the long entrenched philosophies of history of Croce and Gentile, there were in circulation philosophies informed by Christian Democrat tenets, an elusive "spiritualism," a great interest in phenomenology and existentialism, as well as the new-on-the-scene Marxist debates on what history and historicism are and mean (not to speak, of course, of the lively and widely circulated positions of their cousins from up north in Paris).

19. This is argued in Vattimo's preface to the Italian translation of *Wass heist Denken?* (1978, 9–36).

20. This position is explicitly argued in chapter 3, "Towards an Ontology of Decline" (1983, 64), in this volume 17–34.

21. I am thinking of scholars and philosophers such as G. B. Madison, Albert Hofstaedter, Fred Dallmayr, Michael Murray, David Halliburton, Hugh Silverman, Stanley Rosen, all of whom know Vattimo's work and share many common tenets on the interpretation of the subject and of hermeneutics itself.

22. See my analysis of this book in Carravetta 1991a, 215–23.

23. A close American counterpart here could be represented by Margolis' discussion on the *Apeiron*, the Boundless or the "untraversible," in the essay contained in Rockmore and Singer's anthology on anti-foundationalism. The mythic is never developed explicitly by Vattimo, but in its etymological sense of narration is picked up soon after as he unfolds the discursive element, which of course reintroduces us to the problematic of the referent.

24. Recall for instance the collections by Aldo Gargani 1979 and 1985, which signal a bottoming out of the (any) grounds of reason and epistemology in general, and its consequences on any theory of the subject (cf. Carravetta

1989). See as well as the article by Carlo Vinti (in (Rigobello 1988, 147–72), which unravels the history and transformations of subjectivity at the hands of leading philosophers of knowledge such as Bachelard, Polanyi, Popper, and Kuhn. In the context of historical and political interpretations of the subject through the 1980s and the 1990s, see in the bibliography the writings of D'Abbiero, Prandstraller, Zanini, Flores D'Arcais Moravia, and the issue of *Iride* (December 1995, 628–19). For a partial overview of the debate on postmodernism, in which Vattimo intervened often and was as often critiqued (especially by Romano Luperini), see Carravetta 1991b.

25. Vattimo, however, does not interpret *Zarathustra* as poetry, as epic, as allegory, in other words, he does not engage it through the very phenomenon of its rhetoric, its having a particular linguistic structure. For a reinterpretation of the meaning of the style adopted in *Thus Spoke Zarathustra*, see the chapter "Nietzsche and the Rhetoric of the Aphorism" in my book *Prefaces to the Diaphora* (Carravetta 1991a, 17–89).

26. The most significant sampling of the Parisian Nietzsche has been published in English in the anthology *The New Nietzsche* edited by David Allison (1987). For the American ontext, relevant work on Nietzsche had already been done, beside the indefatigable Kaufman, by, Alexander Nehamas, Bernd Magnus, and other authors contained in Robert Solomon 1988.

27. See the historiographical reconstructions of the fortune of Derrida, Lyotard, Lévinas in Italy in Ferraris 1988 and 1990. In the highly politicized Italian cultural panorama of the 1970s and 1980s, much more space was given to thinkers like Foucault, Deleuze, and Guattari, Morin, and the post-Sartre takes on dialectics.

28. Consider in particular the dates of publication of special Nietzsche issues of journals like *il verri, Nuova Corrente, aut aut, rivista di estetica*, as well as several conference proceedings (cf. References). This rich Italian Nietzsche renaissance deserves closer study and reflection.

29. To be sure, to the professional philosophers Heidegger was known from the very start of his career, as can be attested by references to his works in the 1930s by Antonio Banfi, Giovanni Gentile, Nicola Abbagnano, the young Norberto Bobbio and Pareyson, though the problematic political relations between Italy and Germany during the two World Wars did not allow for a more public circulation and discussion of his ideas. On Heidegger's early reception in Italy, see the papers contained in the special issue of *Archivio di Filosofia, La recezione italiana di Heidegger* (1989), edited by Olivetti.

30. The reasons behind this particular turn or epiphenomenon in the genres adopted by professional philosophers is worthy of serious study. We may recall that in France and the United States many an academic critic deserted standardized formal expository writing and turned to novels or more generally

creative constructions. Consider, also, the production, over a twenty-year span, of critics like Roland Barthes, Julia Kristeva, Umberto Eco, and Paolo Valesio.

31. On the rethinking of method as necessary to a "postmodern conception of rationality" see Caputo 1987, 213.

> Our preoccupation with methodology needs to be replaced with a deeper appreciation of *methodos, meta-odos*, which is "the way in which we pursue a matter (*Sache*)," the way we make our way toward the *Sache* . . . in its "retrieved" Heideggerian sense, method is the suppleness by which thinking is able to pursue the matter at hand; it is an acuity which knows its way about . . . [a] keeping underway, in motion.

32. Although in this 1982 article, Vattimo was working with, and perhaps within, the parameters of the philosophy of Gadamer, Habermas, Apel, and Rorty, the basic gist is that there can no longer be a truly or purely empirical or objective knowledge of the other, and this is particularly evident in that discipline that goes the furthest possible, namely anthropology. Against a constantly re-read and we might say updated Heidegger, what is common to both hermeneutics and anthropology is, once again, a trenchant critique of contemporary strong epistemology, and a reconsideration of the role of transcribing, or (re) telling of others. Vattimo's position in this essay brings him into fruitful proximity with theorists like Remo Guidieri, Vincent Crapanzano, Clifford Geertz, Renato Rosaldo, and James Clifford. On the Italian panorama, anthropologists such as Vittorio Lanternari and Carlo Tullio-Altan have dedicated much space to the question of the constitution of the layered, slippery, culture-bound, and untrustworthy subject.

33. On the relationship between literature, the question of the subject, and the inescapable nihilism that is uncovered, see Marco Fortunato's reading of Thomas Mann.

34. I have worked in this direction, rehabilitating rhetoric as intersubjective discourse, in my own *The Elusive Hermes* (Carravetta 2012).

35. "Dialectics, Difference, and Weak Thought" was first read at the 1983 New York University symposium "The Unperfect Actor: Ideology and Hermeneutics in Contemporary Italian Philosophy," and subsequently published in the *Graduate Faculty Philosophy Journal* (1985, vol. 10). The essay appears also as the first chapter of the volume *Il pensiero debole* (1983), now in my English transl. in G. Vattimo and P.A. Rovatti, *Weak Thought* (2012), 39–52. *Il pensiero debole* appeared in the series Contemporary Italian Philosophy as *Weak Thought* (2012). All page references will be to both the Italian version, followed by reference to my English translation.

36. Heidegger's *Verwindung* is the most radical effort to think being in terms of a "taking account of" (*presa d'atto*) which is at once a "taking leave of," for it neither conceives being as a stable structure nor registers and accepts it as the logical outcome of a process. *Verwindung* is the mode in which thought thinks the truth of being as *ueberlieferung* and *geschick* (transmission and destiny-forwarding). In this respect it is synonymous with *Andenken* (memory), which never renders being present but always recalls it as already "gone." (Vattimo and Rovatti 2012, 46–47; Vattimo and Rovatti 1983, 22). For this very reason, it would be absurd to pretend to recover a pure image from the past, or give a perfect account of anything: recollection, interpretation, are always distorted, necessarily, originarily. For a fuller exposition see Vattimo (1987a) and commentary in Carravetta (1991a, 228–31).

37. References are both to original, Vattimo and Rovatti, *Il pensiero debole* (1983) and to the English translation by Carravetta, *Weak Thought* (2012).

38. Stanley Fish writes:

> [T]here is no such thing as a meaning that is specifiable *apart* from the contextual circumstances of its intentional production . . . words (or sentences) in and of themselves do not mean anything and that meaning emerges only within the assumption (whether self-conscious or not) of a speaker who is in a particular situation and who is producing at the moment of utterance a piece of intentional behavior. (Epstein 1991, 11)

39. See the probing essay by Giuseppe Semerari on the factual sociohistorical occurrence of the unfolding of Heidegger's fundamentally Parmenedian understanding of Being. This is linked to Heidegger's testament concerning the prospect that "only a God can save us now" (cf. Semerari 1992, 188; Ferraris 1990).

Author's Preface

1. In particular, "Nietzsche and Beyond the Subject" is from a conference held at the Istituto Italiano per gli Studi Filosofici in Naples in February 1980. "Towards an Ontology of Decline" is the text presented at the seminar on Heideggerian studies organized by the Goethe Institute and the Circolo "L'indiscreto" of Rome in March 1980. "Heidegger and Poetry as the Decline of Language" was read at a seminar held at New York University in March 1979, and published in the volume *Romanticismo, Esistenzialismo, Ontologia della libertà* (Romanticism, existentialism, the ontology of freedom), 1980. (I want to thank the publisher Mursia in Milan for allowing me to reproduce it here.) "Outcomes of Contemporary Hermeneutics" is the text from a seminar held at various universities in

France (Toulouse, Montpellier) and the United States (University of Wisconsin, Milwaukee) in 1980.

2. The most important work by Gadamer is, as is well known, *Truth and Method* (1960), of which there is an Italian version edited and translated by me and published by Fabbri (Milan, 1974) and subsequently reissued by Bompiani (Milan, 1983).

Chapter 1

1. See G. Bataille, *Critique de l'oeil* (Paris: Gallimard, 1972).
2. Deleuze 1985 [1962].
3. I conducted this study in my *Il soggetto e la maschera: Nietzsche e il problema della liberazione* (1974; 2nd ed. 1983).
4. See for example various passages in Bloch, *Das Prinzip Hoffnung* (1959).
5. Nietzsche, *Frammenti Postumi 1885–1887*, in *Opere*, ed. Colli-Montinari (Milan: Adelphi, 1975), vol. 8, t. 1, 126.
6. Ibid., p. 182.
7. Nietzsche, *Twilight of the Idols*, "The Four Great Errors," para. 4.
8. *Frammenti Postumi 1887–88*, in *Opere*, cit., vol. 8, t. 2, 48–49.
9. *Frammenti postumi 1885–87*, cit., 127.
10. Ibid., 199–206.
11. Nietzsche, *Genealogy of Morals*, 3rd essay, sec. 9, 113.
12. Nietzsche, *Beyond Good and Evil*, cit., para. 9.
13. *Genealogy of Morals*, 3rd essay, sec. 24, 151.
14. Nietzsche, *The Gay Science*, book 1, para. 54, 116.
15. Nietzsche, *Frammenti postumi 1885–87*, cit., 297.
16. Nietzsche, *The Gay Science*, cit., aphorism 7.
17. Pautrat, *Versions du soleil*, 1971).
18. *Frammenti Postumi 1885–87*, cit., 297.
19. See Claudio Magris, "Nuova Corrente," in *Dietro quest'infinito* (1979), 79–80nn.

Chapter 2

1. M. Heidegger, *Nietzsche*, 2 vols. (Pfullingen: Neske, 1961).
2. M. Heidegger, *Identität und Differenz* (Pfullingen: Verlag Günther Neske, 1957). I am quoting from the fourth edition. Engl. Trans. by J. Stambaugh, *Identity and Difference*. New York, Harper & Row, 1969.
3. *Opere*, vol. 4, 3, 352; *Human, All Too Human*, II.

4. See H. G. Gadamer, *Truth and Method* (New York: Seabury Press, 1975), 432.

5. M. Heidegger, *Zur Sache des Denkens* (Tübingen: Niemeyer, 1969), 5–6.

6. M. Heidegger, *Being and Time* (New York: Harper and Row, 1962), para. 46.

7. In the sense in which the conferring of the *Grund*, which makes up foundation, has always meant the closure of the series of connections, indeed the constitution of a totality, against regression *in infinitum*.

8. M. Heidegger, *Identität und Differenz*, cit., 38.

9. Ibid., 36–37.

10. Heidegger, *Poetry, Language, Thought*, Engl. trans. A. Hofstadter (New York: Harper, 1971), 180–81.

11. Heidegger, *Identität und Differenz*, 34–35.

12. Ibid., 37. It may be useful to remark that the English translation of Heidegger's passage suggests a different reading with respect to Vattimo's Italian version:

> [The *Er-eignis* is that] ambito in sé oscillante, attraverso il quale uomo ed essere si raggiungono l'un l'altro nella loro essenza, acquistano ció che è loro essenziale in quanto perdono le determinazioni che la metafisica ha loro attribuito. (*Al di là del soggetto*, 68)

> [Das Er-eignis ist der in sich schwingende Bereich, durch den Mensch und Sein einander in ihrem Wesen erreichen, ihr Wesendes gewinnen, indem sie jene Bestimmungen verlieren, die ihnen die Metaphysik geliehen hat.] (102)

The words "schwingende," "Wesen," and "Bestimmungen" have been rendered in English by Joan Stambaugh with "vibrating," "nature," and "qualities," respectively, whereas Vattimo (who could have used the Italian equivalents of these same words), has instead "oscillating," "essence," and "determinations." *Tr.*

13. Ibid., 40.

14. Ibid., 40–41.

15. M. Heidegger, *Der Satz vom Grund* (Pfulligen: Neske, 1957), 186–87. Eng. tr. T. Malick, *The Essence of Reasons*. Evanston: Northwestern University Press, 1969.

Chapter 3

1. M. Heidegger, "Hölderlin and the Essence of Poetry," in *Existence and Being*, ed. Werner Brock (Chicago: Gateway Editions, 1949), 270–91. Also in

M. Heidegger, *Elucidations of Hölderlin's Poetry*, trans. Keith Hoeller (New York: Humanity Books, 2000), 51–65.

2. Originally published in 1968, it was republished in J. Derrida, *Marges de la philosophie* (Paris: Minuit, 1972), 1–29.

3. Heidegger, "Hölderlin."

4. Ibid., 282–83.

5. Ibid.

6. On this distinction between *Anwesen* and *Anwesenlassen*, see Heidegger, *Zur Sache des Denkens*, 5.

7. Heidegger, *Identity and Difference*, 64.

8. M. Heidegger, *Unterweg zur Sprache* (The Way to Language), 157 in *On the Way to Language*, trans. P. D. Hertz (New York, Harper & Row, 1971), 111–36.

9. Ibid.

10. M. Heidegger, "Erläuterungen zu Hölderlins Dichtung," in *Elucidations of Hölderlin's Poetry*, 69. Further references incorporated in the text as EH followed by page number.

11. Originally, I had used Werner Brock's version: "*Physis* is the moving forward and the rising, the disclosing which, by rising, at the same time returns back in its producing (*Hervorgang*), and so it closes upon what time and again gives to each present thing its being present" (translator's comment).

12. M. Heidegger, *Unterwegs* . . . , 216; *On the Way to Language*, 140. It should be noted that the Peter Hertz translation renders this line with "Where words break off no thing may be," whereas Italian translators, more faithful to the original, and perhaps in the wake of Heidegger's reading, insist on retaining the '*ist*' of the first hemistich: "Un 'è' si dà, là dove la parola si infrange." This is not necessarily the most elegant version, but it doesn't betray Hölderlin either. My English version is midway between the two, as "some thing" does give the sense that something "is given" (translator's comment).

13. M. Heidegger, "Language" in *Poetry, Language, Thought*, 199.

14. M. Heidegger, *Unterweg zur Sprache*, 157 ff. On the translation, see translator's note above.

Chapter 4

1. H. G. Gadamer, *Truth and Method*, 432.

2. See F.D.E. Schleiermacher, *Hermeneutik*, 31.

3. Ibid., 87.

4. H. G. Gadamer, *Truth and Method*, 91 ff.

5. Ibid., 267 ff.

6. For a discussion of this tendency of Gadamerian hermeneutics on the basis of critical perspectives no longer entirely valid today, see my article "Estetica ed ermeneutica," in *Rivista di estetica*, no. 1 (1979).

7. See especially K. O. Apel, *Transformation der Philosophie*, 1972, 2 vols. (In partial Italian translation as *Comunità e comunicazione*, Torino, 1977).

8. See especially Habermas, *Logic of the Social Sciences* (Augmented Ital. trans. *Agire comunicativo e logica delle scienze sociali*, Bologna, 1980).

9. K. O. Apel, *Transformation der Philosophie*, cit., and my introduction to the Italian edition.

10. On this aspect has especially insisted American hermeneutics. See E. D. Hirsch, Jr., *Validity in Interpretation* (1967) and most recently, *The Aims of Interpretation* (1976).

11. See H. R. Jauss, *Aesthetische Erfahrung und literarische Hermeneutik*, 1977, vol. I, and the various essays published in French translation, *Pour une esthetique de la reception*, 1978.

12. K. O. Apel, *Comunità e comunicazione*, cit., 172.

13. The term *rimando* means also postponement, putting off, adjournment. I am translating it with "referencing" above all to give the idea that Vattimo is not following a Derridian tack, as we read in the second chapter, and as we gather by the content of his exposition. The sense is that being-there always and constantly harks back to, or makes one think of, a totality which is itself made up of legitimizing structures, pre-established meanings and in short references of all sorts.

14. M. Heidegger, *Identität und Differenz*, 28 ff.

Appendix 1

1. This chapter originally appeared as the lead article in the first issue of *DIFFERENTIA, review of italian thought*, no. 1 (Autumn 1986): 5–22.

2. See in particular my *The Adventures of Difference* (Berkeley: University of California Press, 1994), and chapters 3 and 4 of this volume.

3. See appendix 2 in this volume, originally published in English in *Theory Culture Society*, special issue on Postmodernism (1988) (translator's note).

4. In emblematic fashion, Sartre described this hegemonic position of Marxism in key pages of *Question de Méthode*, which then became the preface to his *Critique of Dialectical Reason* (1960).

5. See J. Habermas and H. G. Gadamer, *Das Erbe Hegels* (Frankfurt: Suhrkamp, 1979): 9–51.

6. I have developed this topic especially in *The End of Modernity* (1980), and must here limit myself to a few remarks. For a more thorough analysis, see my *Il soggetto e la maschera* (1983) and *Introduzione a Nietzsche* (1985).

7. See *Daybreak*, par. 26. Nietzsche's works are hereafter cited by the title and number of the aphorism, or by the number and title of the chapter in

question. The translation I refer to is to the critical edition of the *Opere* edited by G. Colli and M. Montinari (Milan: Adelphi, 1965). The "Posthumous Notes" are also taken from the same edition, with the number of the note, the volume and the page. [Unless otherwise noted, I have made use of the W. Kaufman translations for the English versions of Nietzsche's text reproduced here. *Tr.*]

8. See for example *The Gay Science*, aphorism 35.

9. I have explained at length the reasons for this last adoption in my *Il soggetto e la maschera*, cit. But see also chapters 2 and 3 in this volume.

10. See note 7/60/ in *Opere*, vol. 8, t. 1, 299.

11. Ibid. See also *Beyond Good and Evil*, par. 22.

12. See *The Genealogy of Morals*, III, "What is the Meaning of Ascetic Ideals," ch. 9.

13. *The Genealogy of Morals*, II, ch. 16: "'Guilt,' 'Bad Conscience,' and the Like."

14. Cf. Heidegger, *Saggi e discorsi* (It. trans. G. Vattimo, Milan 1976): 46.

15. See my earlier work *Essere storia e linguaggio in Heidegger* (1963) and *Introduzione a Heidegger* (1985).

16. Cf. Martin Heidegger, *Being and Time*, par. 10, 25, 27.

17. Beside my already cited *Introduzione a Heidegger* (1985), see Ugo M. Ugazio, *Il problema della morte nella filosofia di Heidegger* (Milano: Mursia, 1976).

18. Cf. M. Heidegger, *Der Satz vom Grund* (Pfulligen: Neske, 1957).

19. On this point, see M. Bonola, *Verità e interpretazione nello Heidegger di 'Essere e Tempo'* (Turin: Edizioni di Filosofia, 1983).

20. Cf. Martin Heidegger, *Einführung in die Metaphysik* (1935, but published in 1953), Ital. trans. *Introduzione alla metafisica*, Milan, 1979 [1968], 46–47.

21. See my extensive treatment of this topic in *The Adventures of Difference* (1975).

22. Cf. Martin Heidegger, *Identity and Difference*; Engl. Trans., 37–39.

References

Adorno, Theodor W. *Negative Dialectics*. Trans. E.B.Ashton. New York: Continuum, 1973.
Agazzi, Evandro, ed. *La filosofia della scienza in Italia nel 900*. Milano: D'Angeli, 1989.
Allison, David, ed. *The New Nietzsche*. New York: Dell, 1977; 2nd reprint, MIT Press, 1985.
Apel, K. O. *Transformation der Philosophie*. It. trans. *Comunità e comunicazione*. Turin, 1977.
Artioli, Umberto, and Francesco Bartoli, eds. *Il viandante e la sua ombra. Mappe dell'immaginario e del reale*. Bologna: Cappelli, 1981.
Bataille, G. *Critique de l'oeil*. Paris: Gallimard, 1972.
Bobbio, Norberto. *Profilo ideologico del novecento italiano*. Torino: Einaudi, 1990.
———. *Il problema della guerra e le vie della pace*. Bologna: Il Mulino, 1991, 2nd ed. 2009.
Bodei, Remo. "La speranza dopo il tramonto delle speranze." *Il Mulino* vol. 10, 333 (1991): 5–13.
Braidotti, Rosi. *Soggetto nomade*. Roma: Donzelli, 1995.
Cacciari, Massimo, ed. *Crucialità del tempo. Saggi sulla concezione nietzschiana del tempo*. Napoli: Liguori, 1980.
Cadava, Eduardo, Peter Connor, and Jean-Luc Nancy, eds. *Who Comes After the Subject?* New York: Routledge, 1991.
Caputo, John D. *Radical Hermeneutics. Repetition, Deconstruction, and the Hermeneutic Project*. Bloomington: Indiana University Press, 1987.
Carravetta, Peter. "Italian Philosophy through the War Years." *NEMLA* 36 (2013–2014): 1–38.
———. *The Elusive Hermes: Method, Discourse, Interpreting*. Aurora, CO: Davies Group Publishing, 2012.
———. "Beyond Interpretation? On some perplexities following upon Vattimo's "turn" from hermeneutics." In *Between Nihilism and Politics: The Herme-

neutics of Gianni Vattimo, ed. Silvia Benso and Brian Schroeder, 79–97. Albany: State University of New York Press, 2010.

———. *Prefaces to the Diaphora: Rhetorics, Allegory, and the Interpretation of Postmodernity*. West Lafayette, IN: Purdue University Press, 1991a.

———. "Postmodern Chronicles." *Annali d'italianistica* 9 (1991)b: 32–55.

———. "Repositioning Interpretive Discourse: From *Crisis of Reason* to *Weak Thought*." *DIFFERENTIA, review of italian thought*, no. 2 (1988): 83–126.

———. "An Introduction to the Hermeneutics of Luigi Pareyson." *DIFFERENTIA, review of italian thought* 3/4 (1989): 217–41; revised version, "Form, Person, and Inexhaustible Interpretation." *Parrhesia* 12 (2012): n.p. http://www.petercarravetta.com/wp-content/uploads/2013/02/On-Pareysons-inexhaustible-interpretation1.pdf.

Caruso, Sergio. "L'intersoggettività intrasoggettiva." *Iride* (1995): 648–71.

Crespi, Franco. "La rinascita del soggetto." *Micromega* 3 (1991): 103–13.

D'Abbiero, Marcella. *Per una teoria del soggetto: Marxismo e Psicoanalisi*. Napoli: Guida, 1984.

Dallmayr, Fred R. *Twilight of Subjectivity: Contributions to a Post-Individualist Theory of Politics*. Amherst: University of Massachusetts Press, 1981.

De Grand, Alexander. *The Italian Left in the Twentieth Century*. Bloomington: Indiana University Press, 1989.

Deleuze, Gilles. *Nietzsche and Philosophy*. Chicago: University of Chicago Press, 1985 [1962].

———. *Difference and Repetition*. Eng. tr. P. Patton. New York: Columbia University Press, 1994.

Derrida, Jacques. *Marges de la philosophie*. Paris: Minuit, 1972.

Epstein, William H., ed. *Contesting the Subject*. West Lafayette, IN: Purdue University Press, 1991.

Ferraris, Maurizio. "La morte di Dio e l'eredità di Nietzsche." *aut aut* 236 (March–April 1990): 39–63.

———. *Storia dell'ermeneutica*. Milano: Bompiani, 1988.

———. *La svolta testuale*. Pavia: Cluep, 1984.

Fortunato, Marco. "Figure del Fondo. La filosofia e il soggetto nella *Montagna Incantata* di Thomas Mann." *Itinerari filosofici* (Milano) 2, no. 3 (May–Aug. 1992): 3–28.

Foucault, Michel. *The Order of Things*. New York: Random House, 1973.

Gadamer, Hans Georg. *Truth and Method*. New York: Continuum, 1975.

———. "The Philosophical Foundations of the Twentieth-Century." *Philosophical Hermeneutics*. Eng. trans. David E. Linge. Los Angeles: University of California Press, 1976.

Gargani, Aldo, ed. *La crisi del soggetto. Esplorazione e ricerca del sé nella cultura austriaca contemporanea*. Firenze: la casa USHER, 1985.

———. *Crisi della ragione*. Torino: Einaudi, 1979.
———. *Il sapere senza fondamenti*. Torino: Einaudi, 1975.
Habermas, Jurgen. *Logic of the Social Sciences*. Augmented Ital. trans. *Agire comunicativo e logica delle scienze sociali*, Bologna: Il Mulino, 1980.
———. *Theory of Communicative Action*, vol. 1. Trans. T. McCarthy. Boston: Beacon Press, 1984.
———, and H. G. Gadamer. *Das Erbe Hegels*. Frankfurt: Suhrkamp, 1979.
Hegel, Georg W.F. *The Phenomenology of Spirit*. London: Harper & Row, 1967.
———. *Philosophy of Right*. New York: Cambridge University Press, 1991.
Heidegger, Martin. *Being and Time*. Trans. J. Stambaugh. New York: Harper & Row, 1975.
———. *Essere e tempo*. Ital. trans. Pietro Chiodi. Milano: Longanesi, 1954.
———. *Vorträge und Aufsätze*. Pfullingen: Neske, 1978. Partial trans. E. Lovitt. *The Question Concerning Technology and Other Essays*. New York: Harper, 1977.
———. *Nietzsche*, 2 vols. Pfullingen: Neske, 1961.
———. *Identität und Differenz*. Pfullingen: Verlag Günther Neske, 1957. Engl. Trans. by J. Stambaugh, *Identity and Difference*. New York: Harper & Row, 1969.
———. *Zur Sache des Denkens*. Tübingen: Niemeyer, 1969.
———. *Der Satz vom Grund* (Pfulligen: Neske, 1957). Eng. tr. T. Malick, *The Essence of Reasons*. Evanston: Northwestern University Press, 1969.
———. "Letter on Humanism," in M. Heidegger, *Basic Writings*, ed. D. F. Krell. New York: HarperCollins, 1992, 213–68.
———. *Underwegs zu Sprache*. Eng. trans. P. D. Hertz, *On the Way to Language*. New York: Harper & Row, 1971.
———. *Holzwege*. Eng. trans. J. Young and K. Haynes. *Off the Beaten Track*. Cambridge: Cambridge University Press, 2002.
———. "Hölderlin and the Essence of Poetry." In *Existence and Being*, ed. Werner Brock. Chicago: Gateway Editions, 1949, 270–91.
———. *Elucidations of Hölderlin's Poetry*. Eng. trans. K. Hoeller. New York: Humanity Books, 2000.
———. "The Origin of the Work of Art." In M. Heidegger, Poetry, Language, Thought. Eng. trans. A. Hofstadter. New York: Harper, 1987, 15–88.
Hirsch, E.D., Jr. *Validity in Interpretation*. New Haven: Yale University Press, 1967.
———. *The Aims of Interpretation*. Chicago: University of Chicago Press, 1978.
Jauss, Hans R. *Aesthetische Erfahrung und literarische Hermeneutik*, vol. 1. Munich, 1977. Eng. trans. *Aesthetic Experience and Literary Hermeneutics*. Minneapolis: University of Minnesota Press, 1982.
Lévinas, Emmanuel. *Totality and Infinity*. Eng. trans. Dordrecht, The Netherlands: Kluver Academic Publishers, 1991.
Madison, G. B. *The Hermeneutics of Postmodernity. Figures and Themes*. Bloomington: University of Indiana Press, 1990.

Margolis, Joseph. "The Limits of Metaphysics and the Limits of Certainty." In *Antifoundationalism Old and New*, ed. Rockmore and Singer, 13–40. Philadelphia: Temple University Press, 1992.

Mari, Giovanni, ed. *Moderno postmoderno: soggetto, tempo, sapere nella società attuale*. Milano: Feltrinelli, 1987.

———, ed. *Iride. Filosofia e discussione pubblica* 8, no. 16 (1995): 628–719.

Marramao, Giacomo. *Dopo il leviatano. Individuo e comunità nella filosofia politica*. Torino: Giappichelli, 1995.

———. *L'ordine disincantato*. Roma: Editori Riuniti, 1985.

Moravia, Sergio. "Il soggetto come identità e l'identità del soggetto." *Iride* (Florence), no. 9 (May–Aug. 1992): 78–83.

———. *Analogia del soggetto*. Bari: Laterza, 1991.

Nicolaci, Giuseppe, ed. *La controversia ermeneutica*. Milano: Jaca Book, 1989.

Nietzsche, Fredrick. *Frammenti Postumi 1885–1887*. In *Opere*, ed. Colli-Montinari (Milan: Adelphi, 1975), vol. 8.

———. *The Gay Science*. Trans. W. Kaufman. New York: Vintage, 1974.

———. *Beyond Good and Evil*. Trans. W. Kaufman. New York: Vintage, 1989.

———. *The Will to Power*. Trans. W. Kaufman. New York: Vintage, 1968.

———. *Twilight of the Idols and the Anti-Christ*. Trans. R. J. Hollingdale. New York: Penguin, 1975.

———. *On Truth and Lying in an Extra-moral Sense*. Trans. W. Kaufmann. New York: Penguin, 1973. https://jpcatholic.edu/NCUpdf/Nietzsche.pdf.

———. "The Wanderer and His Shadow" in *Human, All Too Human*. Vol. 2, part 2. Trans. R. J. Hollingdale. New York: Cambridge University Press, 2002.

———. *The Birth of Tragedy AND The Case of Wagner*. Trans. W. Kaufman. New York: Penguin, 1967.

———. *Untimely Meditations*. Trans. R. J. Hollingdale. Cambridge: Cambridge University Press, 1983.

———. *Daybreak*. Trans. R. J. Hollingdale. Cambridge: Cambridge University Press, 1988.

Olivetti, M. M., ed. *La recezione italian di Heidegger*. Padova: Biblioteca dell' "Archivio di Filosofia," 1989.

Pareyson, Luigi. *Existence, Interpretation, Freedom. Selected Writings*. Trans. Paolo Diego Bubbio. Aurora, CO: Davies Group Publishers, 2009.

———. *Estetica. Teoria della formatività*. Firenze: Sansoni, 1954.

———. *Studi sull'esistenzialismo*. Firenze: Sansoni, 1950.

Pasqualotto, Giangiorgio. "Interpretazione interminabile." *Cacciari* (1980): 131–83.

Prandstraller, Gianpaolo. *L'uomo senza certezze e le sue qualità*. Bari: Laterza, 1994.

Rigobello, Armando, ed. *Soggetto e persona. Ricerche sull'autenticità dell'esperienza morale*. Roma: Via dei Genovesi, 1988.

Rockmore, Tom, and Beth J. Singer, eds. *Antifoundationalism Old and New*. Philadelphia: Temple University Press, 1992.

Rovatti, Pier A. *La posta in gioco. Heidegger, Husserl e il soggetto*. Milano: Bompiani, 1987.
Ruggenini, Mario. *Il soggetto e la tecnica. Heidegger interprete 'inattuale' dell'epoca presente*. Roma: Bulzoni, 1977.
Santucci, Aldo. *Esistenzialismo e filosofia italiana*. Bologna: Il Mulino, 1969.
Sartre, Jean Paul. *The Critique of Dialectical Reason*. Trans
Semerari, Fulvio. *Il gioco dei limiti*. Bari: Dedalo, 1993.
Semerari, Giuseppe. "La questione dell'ente-uomo in Heidegger." In *Confronti con Heidegger*, ed. Giuseppe Semerari, 163–89. Bari: Dedalo, 1992.
Schleiermacher, F. D. E. *Hermeneutik*, ed. Kimmerle. Heidelberg, 1959.
Schrag, Calvin O. *Communicative Praxis and the Space of Subjectivity*. Bloomington: University of Indiana Press, 1986.
Singer, Beth. "Metaphysics without Mirrors." In *Antifoundationalism Old and New*, ed. Rockmore and Singer, 189–208. Philadelphia: Temple University Press, 1992.
Smith, Paul. *Discerning the Subject*. Minneapolis: University of Minnesota Press, 1988.
Solomon, Robert and Kathleen Higgins, eds. *Reading Nietzsche*. New York: Oxford University Press, 1988.
Tullio-Altan, Carlo. *Soggetto simbolo e valore. Per un'ermeneutica antropologica*. Milano: Feltrinelli, 1992.
Vattimo, Gianni. "Filosofia, metafisica, democrazia." *Rivista di filosofia* 88, no. 1 (April 1997): 117–26.
———. *Oltre l'interpretazione*. Bari: Laterza, 1994. Engl. trans., *Beyond Interpretation*.
———. *The Adventures of Difference: Philosophy after Nietzsche and Heidegger*. Trans. C. P. Blamires and T. Harrison. Cambridge: Polity Press, 1993.
———. "Hermeneutics as Koine." *Theory, Culture, & Society* 5, no. 2–3 (1988): 7–17.
———. "*Verwindung*: Nihilism and the Postmodern in Philosophy," *SubStance* 16.2, no. 53 (1987): 7–17.
———. "Ermeneutica e secolarizzazione." *AUT AUT*, no. 213 (May–June 1986): 17–27.
———. *Introduzione a Heidegger*. Bari: Laterza, [1980 and 1981] 1985.
———. *La fine della modernità*. Milano: Garzanti, 1985.
———, and P. A. Rovatti. *Il pensiero debole*. Milano: Feltrinelli, 1983. *Weak Thought*. Trans. P. Carravetta. Albany: State University of New York Press, 2012.
Vinti, Carlo. "Struttura della soggettività e nozione di persona nell'epistemologia contemporanea." A. Rigobello, *Soggetto e persona*, 147–70.
Walker, Cheryl. "Persona Criticism and the Death of the Author," In *Contesting the Subject*, ed. Epstein, 109–22. West Lafayette, IN: Purdue University Press, 1991.

Wurzer, Wilhelm S. "Nietzsche and the Problem of Ground." In *Antifoundationalism Old and New*, ed. Rockmore and Singer, 127–42. Philadelphia: Temple University Press, 1992.
Zanini, Adelino. *Il moderno come residuo. Dieci lemmi*. Roma: Pellicani, 1989.
———. *Filosofie del soggetto. Soggettività e costituzione*. Palermo: La palma, 1982.

References for Gianni Vattimo's Works

1997. "Filosofia, metafisica, democrazia." *Rivista di filosofia* 88. no. 1 (April 1997): 117–26.
1994. *Oltre l'interpretazione*. Bari: Laterza. Engl. Trans. *Beyond Interpretation*.
1993. *The Adventures of Difference: Philosophy after Nietzsche and Heidegger*. Trans. C.P. Blamires and T. Harrison. Cambridge: Polity Press.
1988. "Hermeneutics as Koine." *Theory, Culture, & Society* 5, no. 2–3: 7–17.
1987a. "*Verwindung*: Nihilism and the Postmodern in Philosophy," *SubStance* 16.2, no. 53 (1987): 7–17.
1986. "Ermeneutica e secolarizzazione." *AUT AUT*, no. 213 (Maggio-giugno): 17–27.
1985a [1981 and 1980]. *Introduzione a Heidegger*. Bari, Laterza.
1985b. *La fine della modernità*. Milano, Garzanti.
1985c. "L'essenza mortale della letteratura." *Sigma* 16, no. 1: 61–66.
1984. *Al di là del soggetto*. Milano, Feltrinelli.
1982. "Difference and Interference: On the Reduction of Hermeneutics to Anthropology." *Res* 4, 85–91.
1980 [1975]. *Le avventure della differenza*. Milano, Garzanti. Engl. Trans. 1993.
1978. "Prefazione" to the translation of M. Heidegger's *Wass heist Denken? Che cosa significa pensare?* Milano: Sugarco Edizioni.
1974. *Il soggetto e la maschera. Nietzsche e il problema della liberazione*. Milano, Bompiani. 2nd ed., 1983.
1968. *Schleiermarcher, filosofo dell'interpretazione*. Milano, Mursia.
1963. *Essere storia e linguaggio in Heidegger*. Torino, Edizioni di "Filosofia".

Index of Names

Abbagnano, Nicola, 96n
Adorno, Theodor, xxxii, xl, 47, 88
Agazzi, Evandro, 94n
Althusser, Luis, 85
Apel, Karl Otto, 20, 53–60, 62, 63, 64, 69, 84, 93n, 97n, 102n
Aristotle, xiii, 19, 51, 94

Bachelard, Gaston, 96n
Balibar, Etienne, xxiv
Banfi, Antonio, 96n
Barthes, Roland, xix, xxi, 97n
Bataille, George, 1, 99n
Bateson, Gregory, 16
Beckett, Samuel, 47
Benjamin, Walter, 29
Benveniste, Emile, xxi
Bloch, Ernst, xl, 3, 41, 99n
Bobbio, Norberto, xxix, 94n, 96n
Braidotti, Rosi, xxiv
Brock, Werner, 100n
Bubbio, Paolo D., 94n

Cacciari, Massimo, xvii, xviii
Cadava, Eduardo, xxiv
Caputo, John, 97n
Carravetta, Peter, ix, 93n–98n
Chiodi, Pietro, xviii
Chomsky, Noam, xxxvi

Clifford, James, 97n
Colli, Giorgio, xvii, 99n, 103n
Comolli, Gianpiero, xviii
Connor, Peter, xxiv
Copernicus, 20, 21
Crapanzano, Vincent, 97n
Croce, Benedetto, xiii, xvii, 95n

Dabbiero, Marcella, 96n
Dallmayr, Fred, 95n
De Certeau, Michel, xxiv
De Grand, Alexander, 94n
Deleuze, Gilles, 2, 3, 11, 38, 39, 93n, 96n, 99n
Derrida, Jacques, xix, xxi, xxv, 35, 38, 39, 69, 84, 86, 93n, 95n, 96n, 102n
Descartes, René (Cartesian), x, 57, 58, 88
Dilthey, Wilhelm, 50, 51, 54, 69

Eco, Umberto, 86, 97n
Epstein, William, 98n

Ferraris, Maurizio, 86, 96n, 98n
Fish, Stanley, xxiv, 98n
Fortunato, Marco, 97n
Foucault, Michel, ix, xix, xxv, 69, 84, 93n, 96n

112 / Index of Names

Freud, Sigmund, 88

Gadamer, Hans Georg, xviii, xxi, 19,
  22, 38, 49, 52–57, 63, 69, 83, 84,
  86–90, 94, 97n, 99–102nn
Gargani, Aldo, xviii, 94n, 95n
Geertz, Clifford, 97n
Gentile, Giovanni, xiii, 95n, 96n,
  103n
George, Stefan, 48
Gramsci, Antonio, 9
Guidieri, Remo, 97n

Habermas, 16, 20, 53–57, 59, 60,
  62, 63, 69, 84, 88–90, 93n, 97n,
  102n
Halliburton, David, 95n
Hegel, Georg W. F., xxxii, xxvii, 2, 3,
  52, 53, 57, 59, 68, 87, 88, 93n
Heidegger, Martin, x, xii–xxix, xxi,
  xxii, xxiv, xxx, xxxv–xxxvii, xxxix,
  xl, 1, 8, 17–19, 21–33, 35–49, 51,
  54, 56, 57, 59, 60, 62–64, 67–70,
  75–82, 86, 88, 90–92, 93–103nn
Hertz, Peter, 101n
Hirsch, E. D. Jr., 102n
Hofstaedter, Albert, 95n, 100n
Hölderlin, Friedrich, xv, xxxv, 35, 43,
  45, 56, 65, 100n
Husserl, Edmund, 38, 55, 59, 61,
  88, 93n

Jauss, Hans R., 56, 57, 59, 69, 102n

Kant, Immanuel, xiv, xxiii, xxiv,
  xxxvi, 19, 20, 21, 26, 27, 31, 32,
  37, 42, 53–55, 57, 58, 62–64, 74,
  89, 90, 93n
Kierkegaard, Soren, xxi, 61
Kristeva, Julia, 97n

Lacan, Jacques, 38, 39
Lanternari, Vittorio, 97n
Lévinas, Emmanuel, xxxv, 96n
Lévi-Strauss, Claude, xix, 85
Lukács, Gyorg, xvii, xxxviii

Madison, G.P., xxi, 94n, 95n
Magris, Claudio, 99n
Mann, Thomas, 97n
Margolis, Joseph, 95n
Marx, Karl, xiii, xvii, xviii, xix, xxxii–
  xxxv, xxxvii, xl, 2, 3, 60, 69, 83,
  93–95nn, 102n
Masini, Ferruccio, xvii
Mazzarella, Eugenio, xviii
Montinari, Martino, xvii, 99n, 103n
Murray, Michael, 95n
Musil, Robert, 15

Nancy, Jean-Luc, xxiv
Nietzsche, Friedrich, ix, x, xii–xiv,
  xvi–xviii, xxi, xxiv, xxv, xxx, xxxvi–
  xl, 1–16, 17, 19–21, 24, 25, 27,
  30, 32, 47, 67–82, 93, 95, 96, 98,
  102n, 103n

Olivetti, Marco, 95n, 96n

Pareyson, Luigi, xiii, xx, 69,
  94–96nn, 106n
Parmenides, xxxix
Pasqualotto, Giangiorgio, xvii, xxv
Pautrat, Bernard, 13, 99n
Peirce, C.S., 58, 86
Penzo, Giorgio, xvii
Perniola, Mario, xviii
Plato, xiii, xxix, xxx–xxxii, xxxv–xxx-
  viii, 3, 6, 33, 48
Polanyi, Michael, 96n
Popper, Karl, 96n

Index of Names / 113

Prandstreller, Giampaolo, 96n

Rella, Franco, xviii
Ricoeur, Paul, 49, 56, 57, 59, 69, 84, 92n, 93n, 94n
Rigobello, Armando, 96n
Rockmore, Tom, 95n
Rorty, Richard, xxiv, 69, 97n
Rosaldo, Renato, 97n
Rosen, Stanley, 95n
Rousseau, Jacques, 13, 14
Rovatti, Pier Aldo, xviii, xxii, xxiv, 97n, 98n
Ruggenini, Ruggiero, xviii

Santucci, Aldo, 94n
Sartre, Jean-Paul, xxxviii, 85, 96n, 102n
Saussure, Ferdinand de, 41, 51, 86
Schleiermacher, F. D. E., 50, 51, 52, 55, 62, 69
Schopenhauer, Arthur, 74
Schrag, Calvin, 93n

Semerari, Fulvio, xvii, 98n
Severino, Emanuele, xvii
Silverman, Hugh, vii, 95n
Simmel, Georg, 29
Singer, Beth, 95n
Sini, Carlo, xviii
Stambaugh, Joan, 100n

Tullio-Altan, Carlo, 97n

Valesio, Paolo, 97n
Vattimo, Gianni, x, xi–xxv, xxvii, xxix, 89, 93–98nn, 102–3nn
Vinti, Carlo, 96n
Vitiello, Ciro, xviii

Walker, Cheryl, xix, xx
Weber, Max, xxxii, 78
West, Cornel, xxiv
Wittgenstein, Ludwig, xxix, 49, 55, 56, 63

Zecchi, Stefano, xviii

Index of Terms

Abgrund, 31, 33, 42, 46, 62
Actualitas, xxvii

Befindlichkeit, 21, 25, 44
Begründung, 19

Cogito, x

Dasein, xxiii, 20, 21, 22, 25, 26, 27, 75, 76, 77, 78
Deconstruction, x, xxi, 24, 86
Degrounding, xvii, xxvii, xxxvi, 21, 23, 24, 26, 27, 39, 41, 43, 45–48, 52, 53, 57, 59, 60, 65
Democracy, xxxiii
Dialectics, xvii, xxi, xxii, xxiv, xxvii, xxxviii, xxix, xl, 2, 4, 88, 96n
Differenz, xvi; references to Heidegger's *Identität und Differenz*, 18, 27, 29, 30, 31, 63, 99n, 101n, 102n
Dissolution, xi, xxxviii, xxxix, 8, 10, 15, 35, 70, 71, 75, 78, 82, 84, 85

Ego, x, xxv, 72, 88
Einfühlen, xxvi
Ereignis, 27–32, 76, 78, 100n
Erörterung, xvi
Essence, xiv, 2, 6, 9, 12, 19, 29, 31, 35, 47, 71, 76, 80, 89; of poetry, xx, 35, 47, 48; of subjectivity, xxi; of being, xxiii; of humans, 11, 79; of hermeneutics, 14, 59; of technology, 27, 31, 82

Figura, x, xvi, xix, xxv, 42, 44
Foundation, x, xiii, xxvi, 5, 16, 19–22, 24–28, 30–33, 35, 39, 42, 43, 45–47, 50–53, 57, 59, 60–65, 70, 71, 73, 75, 76, 78, 79, 80, 82, 90

Gemeinwesen, xxxii
Gestell, 27–32, 79, 80
Geviert, xv, 29, 47
Grund, 5, 19, 20, 21, 22, 24, 28, 30–33, 42; in later Heidegger, 76, 77

Heraus-forderung, 28
Hermeneia, xxxiii
Hermeneutics, x; in Apel, 54–57, 59, 60, 62, 93n; and American continental philosophy, 94n; and being, 92; consequences for, xii, xxvii; and phenomenology, xii, xiii; authenticity of, xvi, xviii; as koine, xviii, 69, 83–93; and anthropology, xix, 97n; and secularization, xx; and postmodernity, xxi; outlook

Hermeneutics *(continued)*
for, xxi, xxiv, xxv, xxvi; and metaphysics, 9; Nietzsche's, 10, 12–14; in Habermas, 16, 59, 60, 62, 93n; in Heidegger, 57, 59, 63; 64, 69; and history, 91; in Gadamer, 19, 54, 83; in G. B. Madison 94n; non-transcendental, 91; outcomes of contemporary, 49–65, 84, 89; and Ricoeur, 94n; in Schleiermacher, 50–52, 53, 62

Kehre (turn), xiv, 26; in Nietzsche, 13

Marxism, xiii, xvii, xviii, xix, xxxii–xxxv, xxxvii, xl, 2, 60, 69, 83, 94n, 95n, 102n

Metaphysics, xiii, xiv, xxii, xxix, 3, 5, 6, 8, 11, 13, 14, 16, 18, 24, 27, 33, 38, 79, 80, 82, 86, 91, 95n; anti-metaphysical xvi, 9; in Apel, 63; in Heidegger, 19, 21, 29, 41, 48, 60, 62, 79, 80, 86, 90, 91, 92, as history of being, 17, 18, 26, 30, 31, 91; in Nietzsche, 68, 75, 80; post-metaphysical xi, xxii, 81

Modernity, x, xxi, 16

Nihilism, xi, 6, 7, 8, 20, 21, 24, 25, 33, 68, 69, 70, 71, 73, 75, 78, 93n, 97n
Noetic, xxiii

Ontology, 14, 21, 60, 61, 73, 78, 98n; of actuality xxvii; of art xiv; of decline xvi, xxxix, 17–34; in Heidegger, 23; hermeneutic, xxiv, 15, 16, 17, 19, 54; and nihilism 78; weak xxiii

Overman, xxxvii, xxxviii, 1, 2, 3, 8, 10, 12, 15, 16, 73, 74, 75, 80, 81. See also *Übermensch*

Pietas, xxiii, 18
Postmodernity/late Modern, x, xxi, xxxi, xxxii, xxxvii, 16, 67, 70, 81

Res cogitans, xxv

Seinfrage, xvi
Sfondamento, xxxvi, 21, 26, 43, 46, 59, 60, 64, 74. See also degrounding
Subjectivity, x; ahistorical nature, 89; cannot escape from, xxv, xxvii; crisis of, 73; decline of, 47, 48; different theories of, xvi–xxii, xxiv; idealization of, 58, 67; liberation from, xxxviii; metaphysical nature of, 73–82; and the overman, 73; potential in rethinking, xi; relation to *Dasein*, 76; transcendental, 93; transformations, of 96; unmasking of, 70–71; untenability of 76–77; in Vattimo's background, xii

Theoros, x

Uber-lieferung, xxiv, 32, 33, 38, 65, 77, 78
Übermensch, xx, xxxvii, 1, 2, 3, 6, 8–16, 73. See also overman
Ursprung, xv

Value/values, xi, xxi, xxx–xxxv, xxxvii–xxxix, 2, 3, 9, 11, 12, 14, 21, 24, 25, 26, 29, 32, 70, 73, 78
Verwindung, xi, xxii, 92, 98n

Weak/weakening, xii, xiv, xxi–xxv, xxxix, 16, 20, 32, 33, 61, 97n, 98n

Zarathustra, xvii, xxv, xxvii, 1, 2, 11, 73, 96n

www.ingramcontent.com/pod-product-compliance
Lightning Source LLC
Chambersburg PA
CBHW030828230426
43667CB00008B/1429